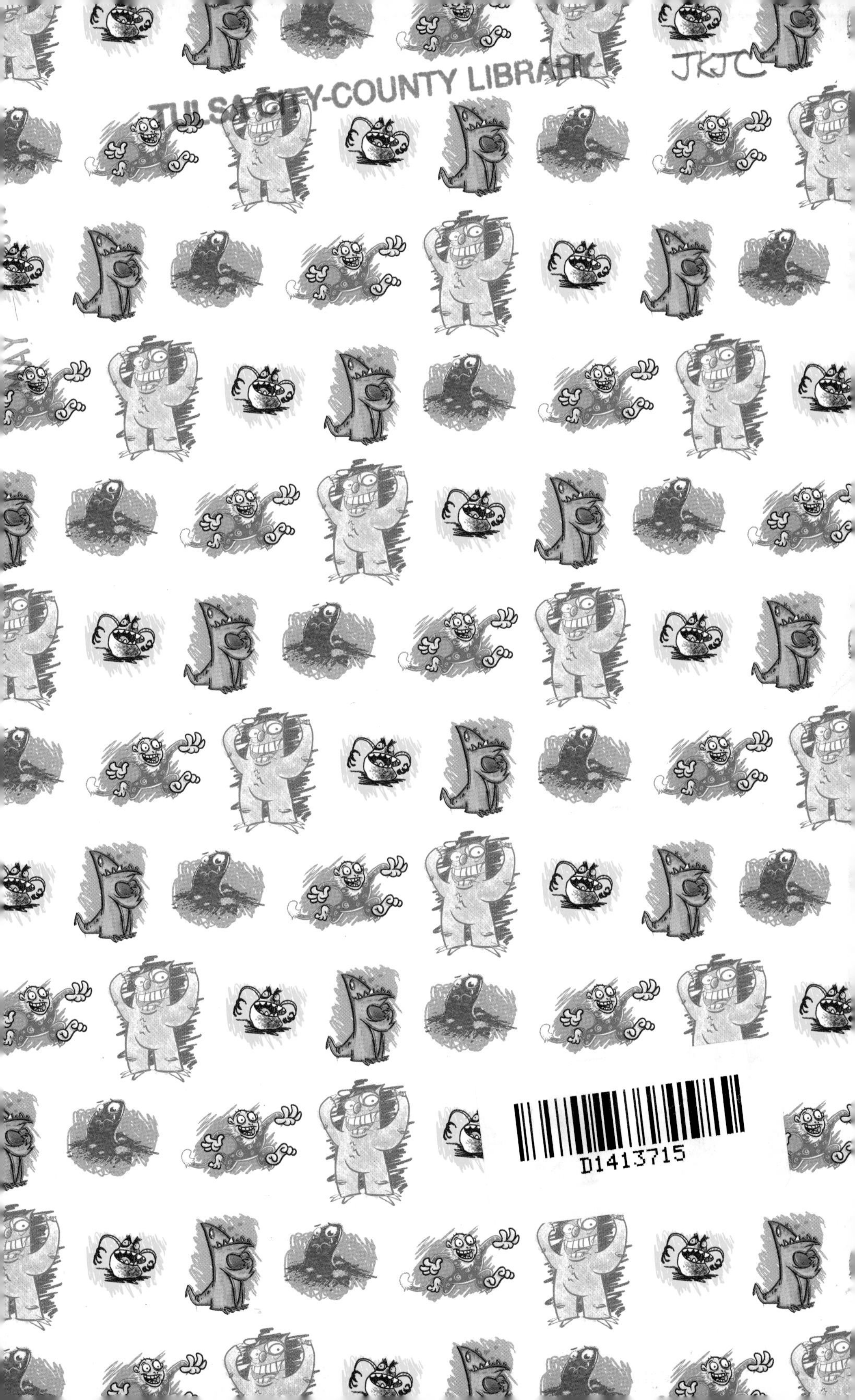

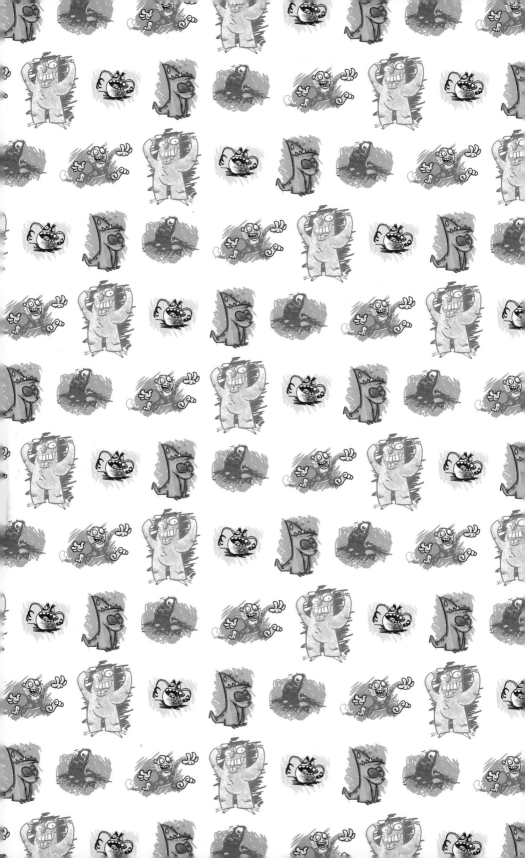

SKETCH MONSTERS

THE NEW KID

AN ONI PRESS PUBLICATION

THE NEW KID

by

JOSHUA WILLIAMSON

&

VINNY NAVARRETE

logo designed by
VINNY NAVARRETE

book designed by
KEITH WOOD

edited by
JILL BEATON

To Cordelia. The best small dog and sidekick a man could ever have.
Just please stop pooping in the house.
—Joshua

I dedicate this book to a cat named Jake. Thank you for
hanging out with me as I worked into the wee-hours of
countless mornings. "Good boy, Jake."
—Vinny

Oni Press, Inc.

PUBLISHER Joe Nozemack
EDITOR IN CHIEF James Lucas Jones
ART DIRECTOR Keith Wood
DIRECTOR OF BUSINESS DEVELOPMENT George Rohac
DIRECTOR OF SALES AND MARKETING Tom Shimmin
EDITOR Jill Beaton
EDITOR Charlie Chu
DIGITAL PREPRESS LEAD Troy Look
GRAPHIC DESIGNER Jason Storey
ADMINISTRATIVE ASSISTANT Robin Herrera

onipress.com • thejoshuawilliamson.com • vinnyville.carbonmade.com

Oni Press, Inc.
1305 SE M.L.K. Jr. Blvd.
Portland, OR 97214
USA

First edition: February 2012

ISBN 978-1-62010-012-7

Library of Congress Control Number: 2012953354

1 3 5 7 9 10 8 6 4 2

Printed in China.

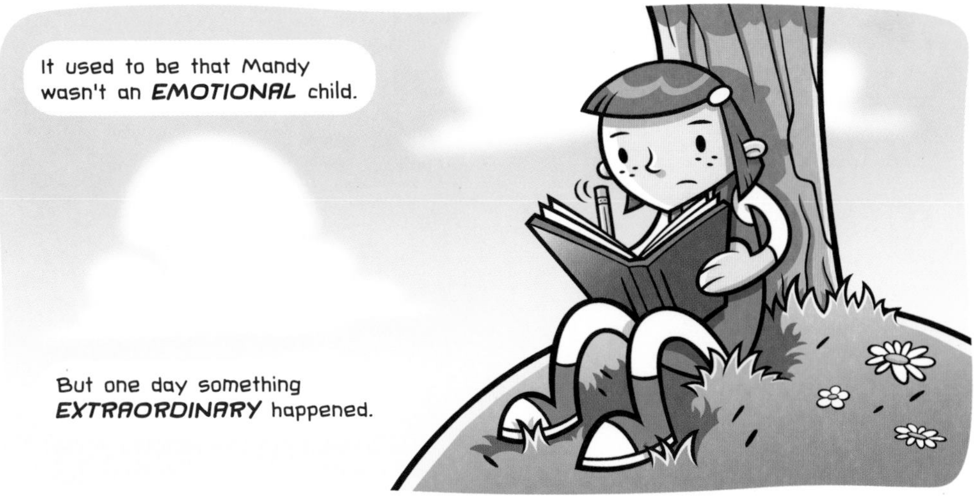
It used to be that Mandy wasn't an EMOTIONAL child.
But one day something EXTRAORDINARY happened.

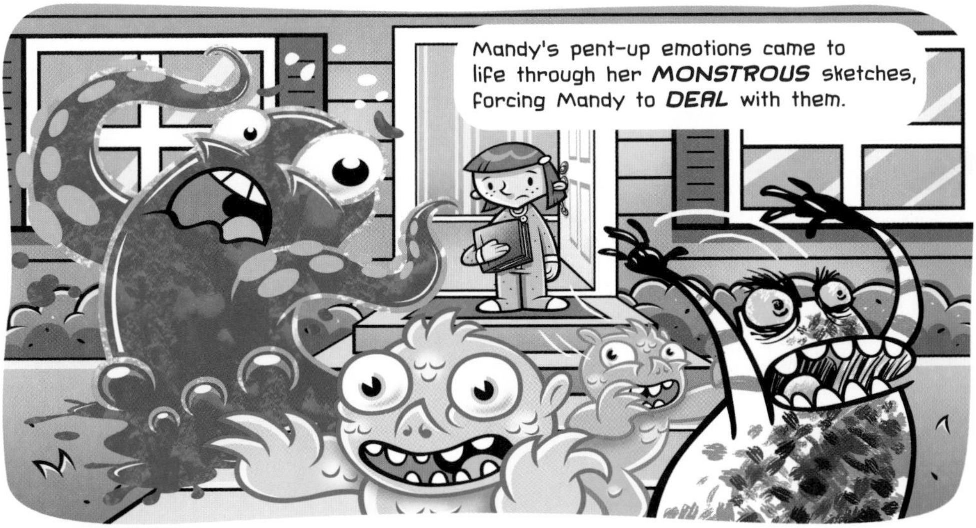
Mandy's pent-up emotions came to life through her MONSTROUS sketches, forcing Mandy to DEAL with them.

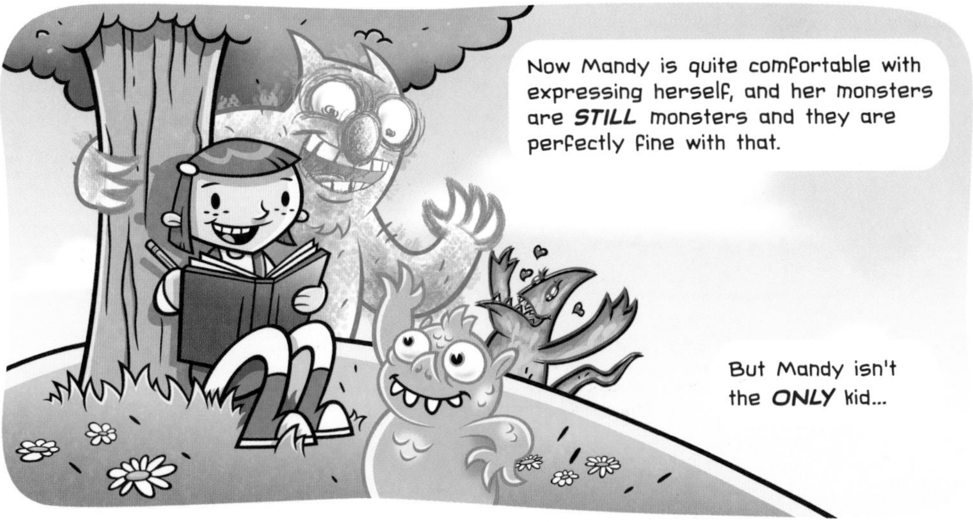
Now Mandy is quite comfortable with expressing herself, and her monsters are STILL monsters and they are perfectly fine with that.
But Mandy isn't the ONLY kid...

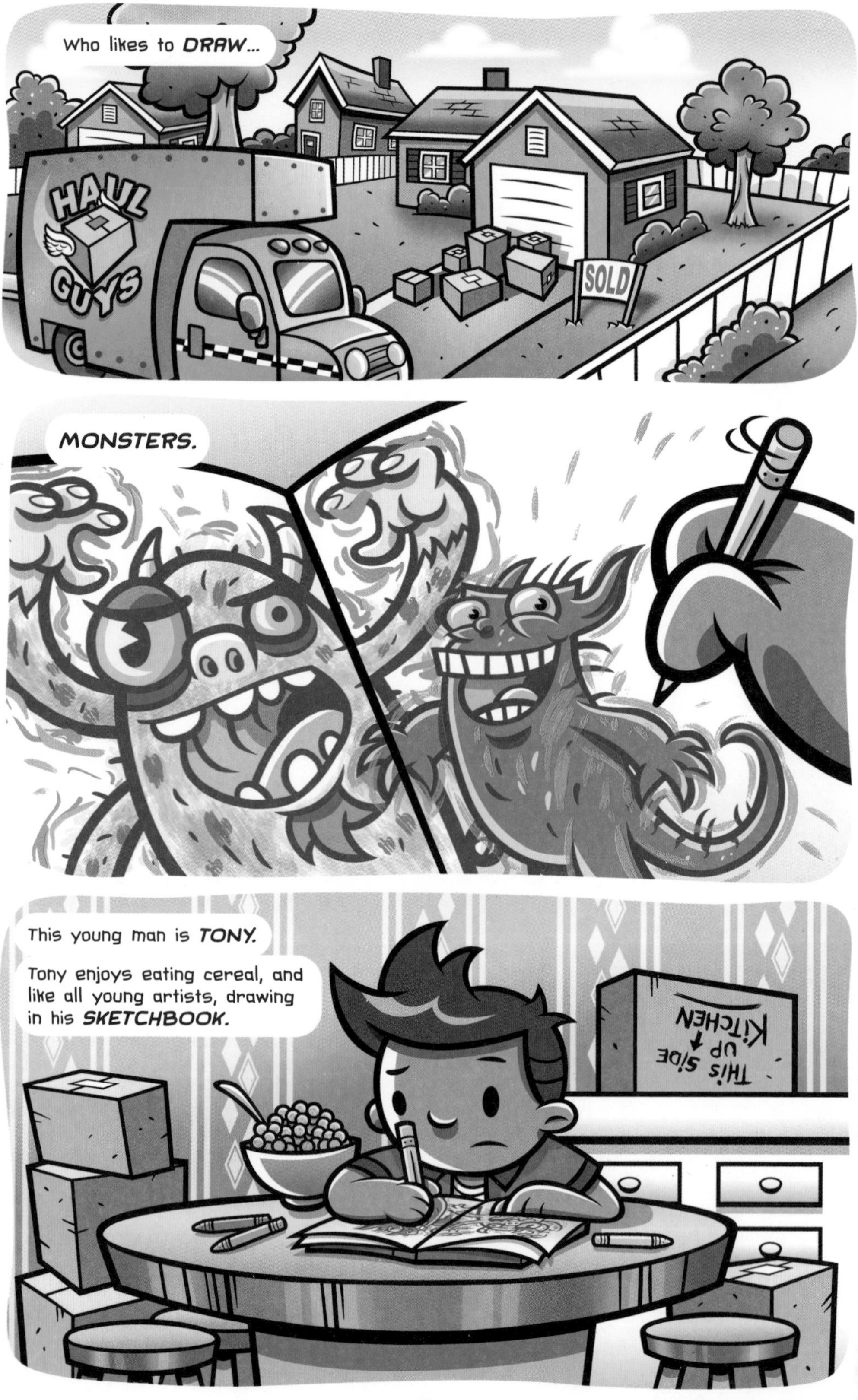
Who likes to DRAW...
HAUL GUYS
SOLD
MONSTERS.
This young man is TONY.
Tony enjoys eating cereal, and like all young artists, drawing in his SKETCHBOOK.
KITCHEN
THIS SIDE UP

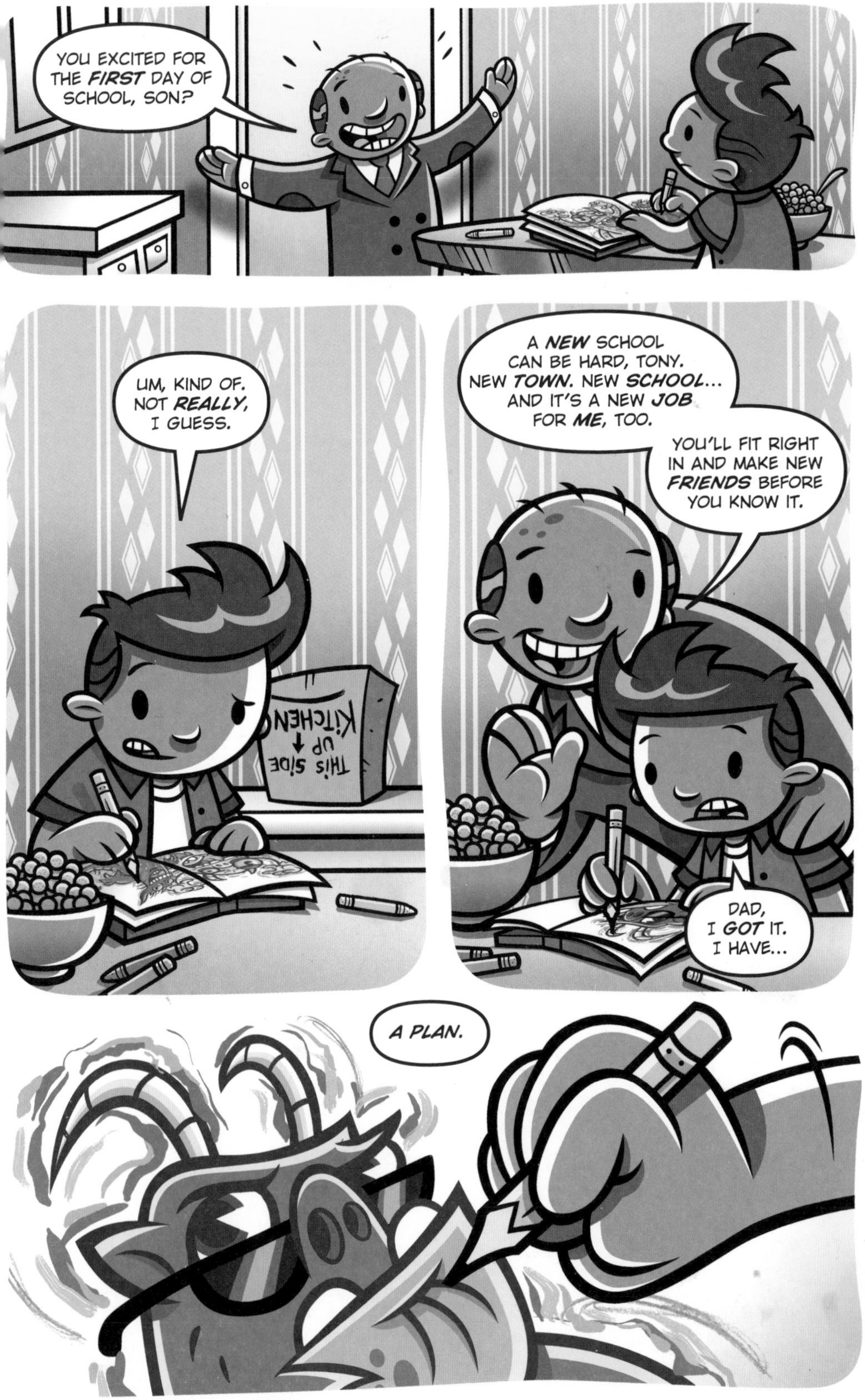
YOU EXCITED FOR THE *FIRST* DAY OF SCHOOL, SON?
UM, KIND OF. NOT *REALLY,* I GUESS.
THIS SIDE UP KITCHEN
A *NEW* SCHOOL CAN BE HARD, TONY. NEW *TOWN.* NEW *SCHOOL*... AND IT'S A NEW *JOB* FOR *ME,* TOO.
YOU'LL FIT RIGHT IN AND MAKE NEW *FRIENDS* BEFORE YOU KNOW IT.
DAD, I *GOT* IT. I HAVE...
A PLAN.

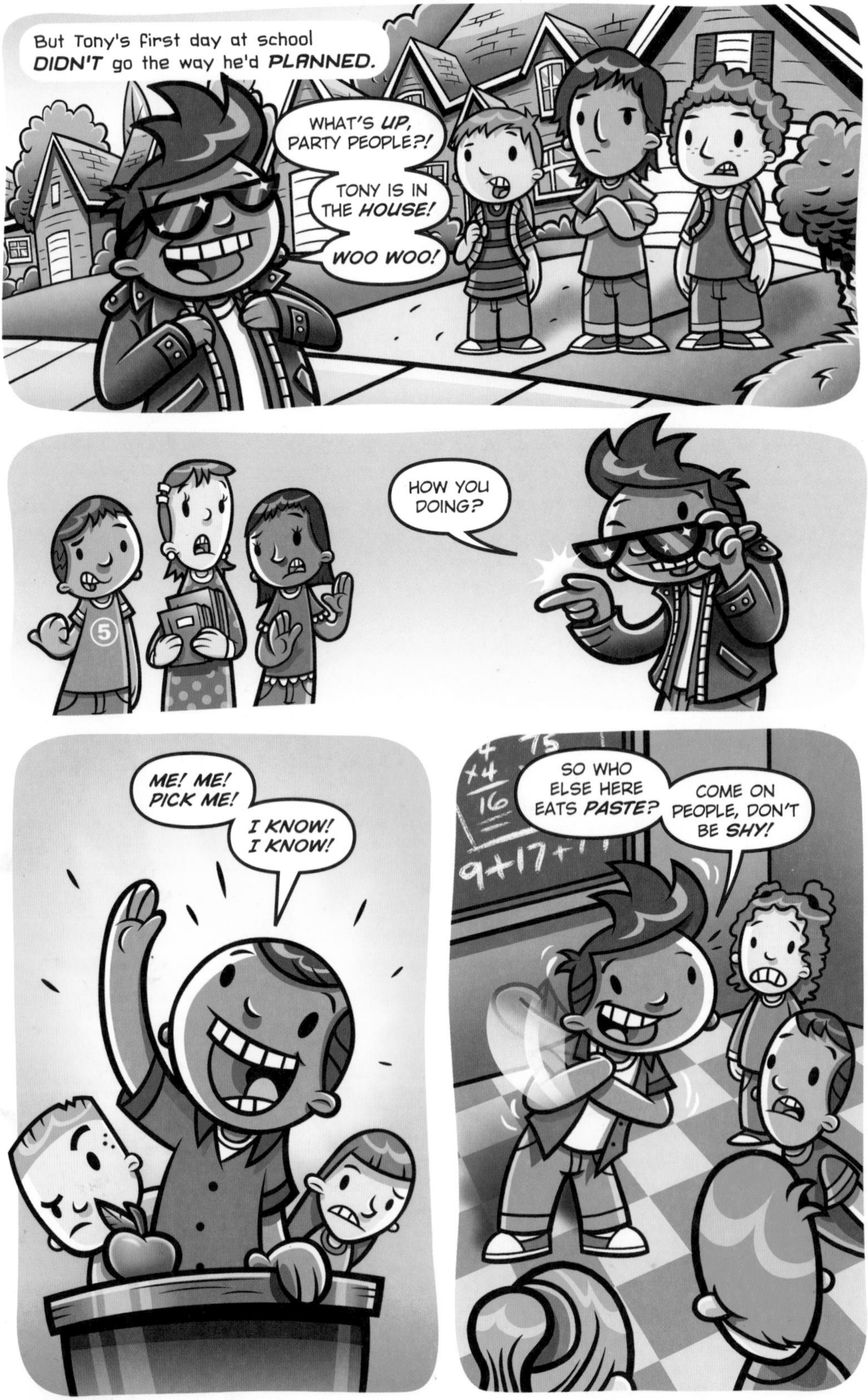
But Tony's first day at school *DIDN'T* go the way he'd *PLANNED.*
WHAT'S *UP,* PARTY PEOPLE?!
TONY IS IN THE *HOUSE!*
WOO WOO!
HOW YOU DOING?
ME! ME! PICK ME!
I KNOW! I KNOW!
SO WHO ELSE HERE EATS *PASTE?*
COME ON PEOPLE, DON'T BE *SHY!*

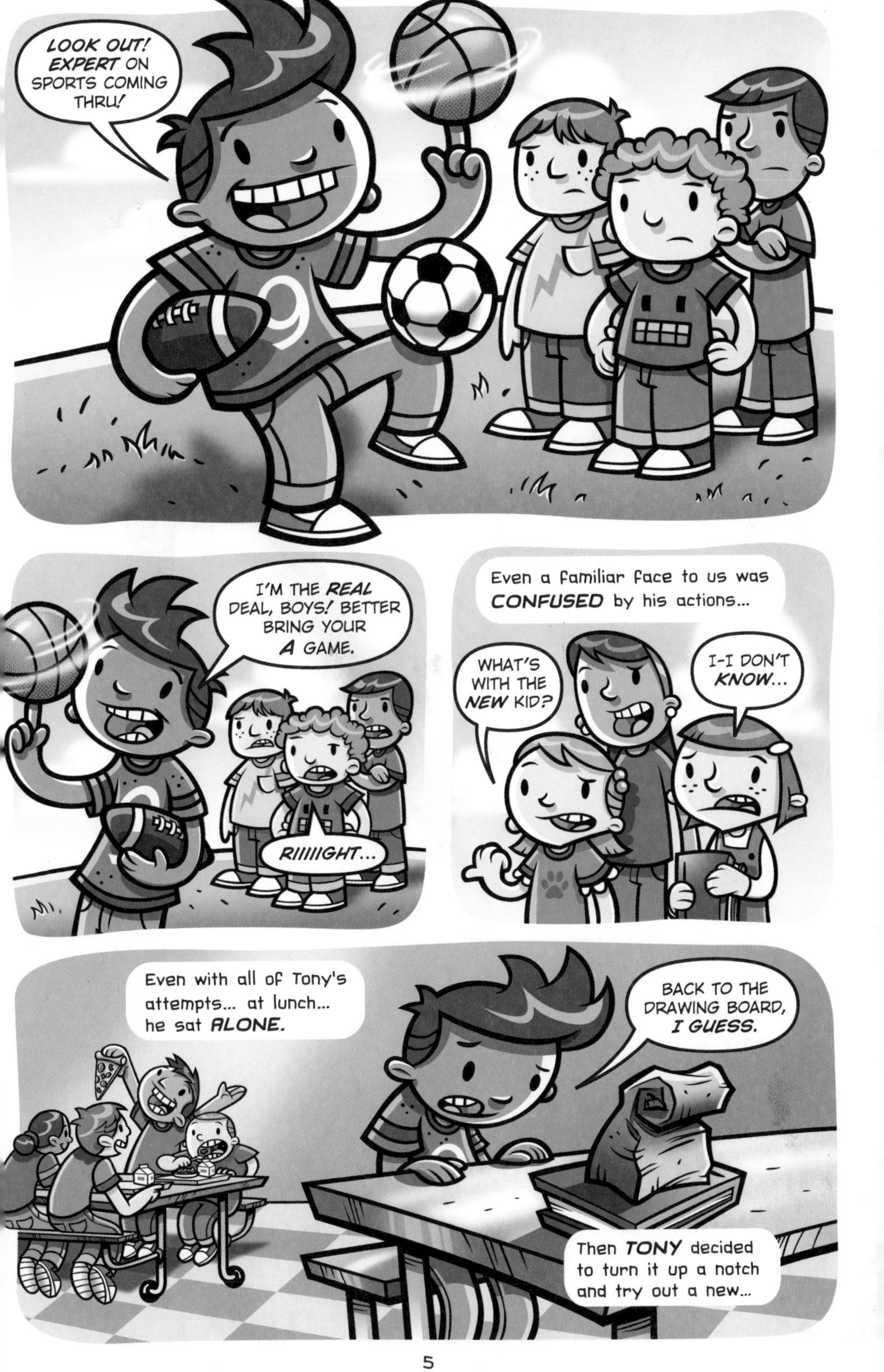
LOOK OUT! EXPERT ON SPORTS COMING THRU!
I'M THE REAL DEAL, BOYS! BETTER BRING YOUR A GAME.
RIIIIIGHT...
Even a familiar face to us was CONFUSED by his actions...
WHAT'S WITH THE NEW KID?
I-I DON'T KNOW...
Even with all of Tony's attempts... at lunch... he sat ALONE.
BACK TO THE DRAWING BOARD, I GUESS.
Then TONY decided to turn it up a notch and try out a new...

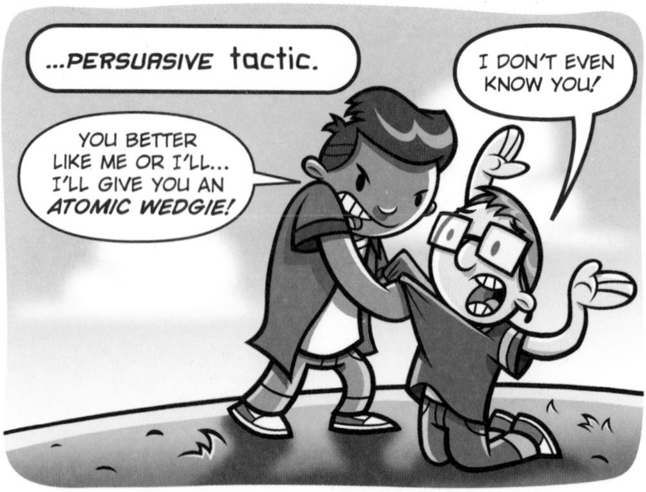
...PERSUASIVE tactic.
YOU BETTER LIKE ME OR I'LL... I'LL GIVE YOU AN ATOMIC WEDGIE!
I DON'T EVEN KNOW YOU!

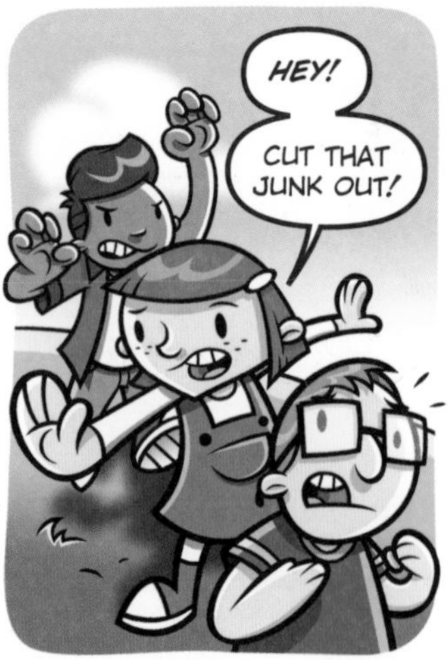
HEY!
CUT THAT JUNK OUT!

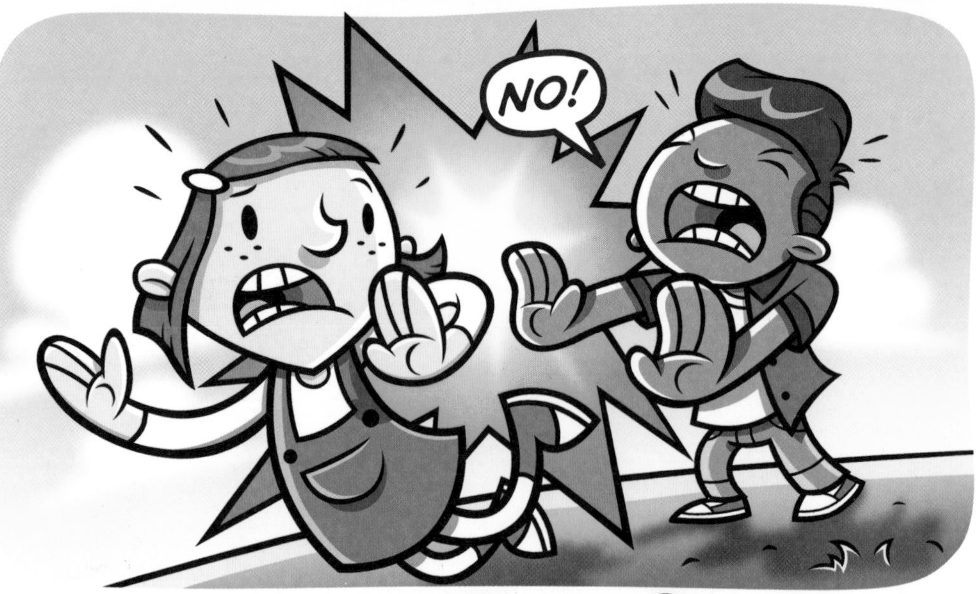
NO!

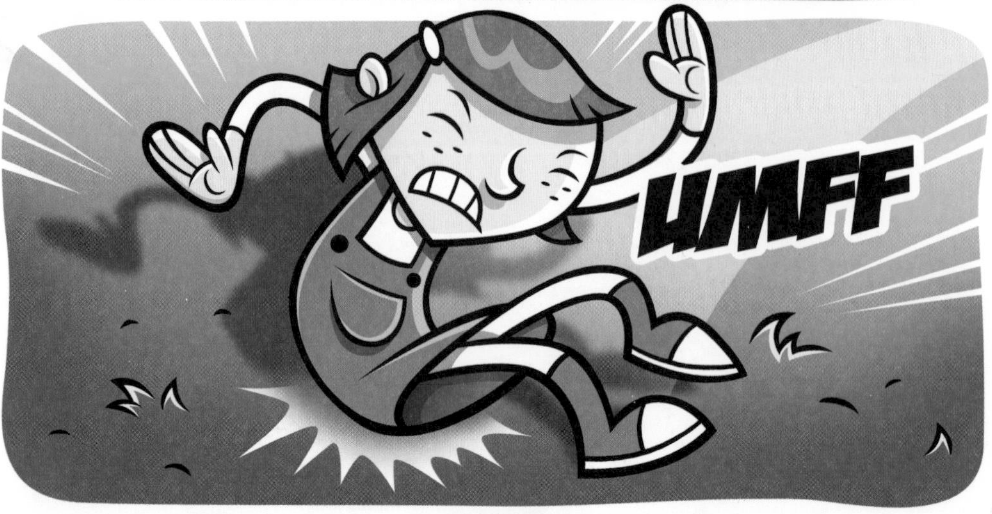
UMFF

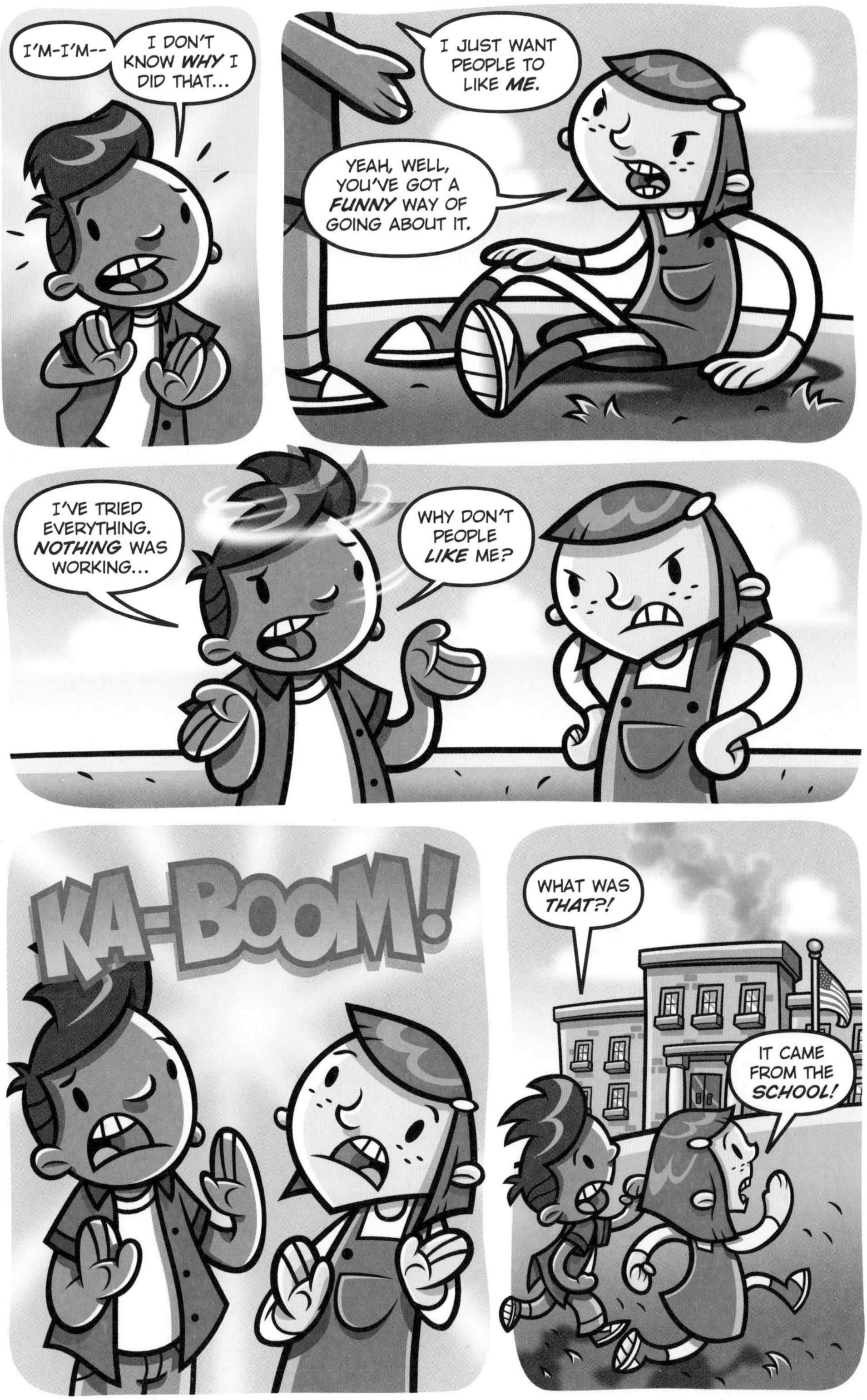
I'M-I'M--
I DON'T KNOW WHY I DID THAT...
I JUST WANT PEOPLE TO LIKE ME.
YEAH, WELL, YOU'VE GOT A FUNNY WAY OF GOING ABOUT IT.
I'VE TRIED EVERYTHING. NOTHING WAS WORKING...
WHY DON'T PEOPLE LIKE ME?
KA-BOOM!
WHAT WAS THAT?!
IT CAME FROM THE SCHOOL!

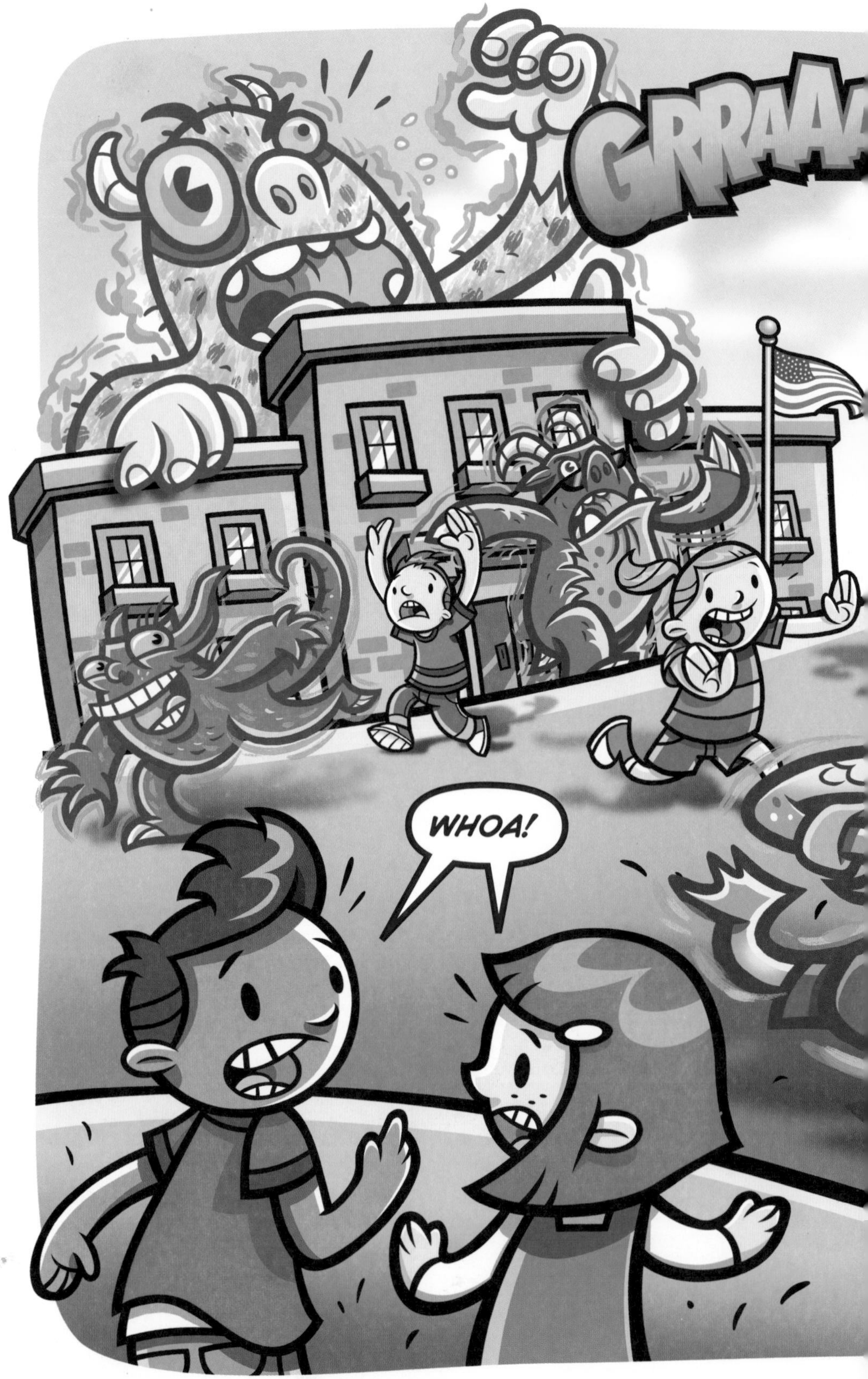
GRRAAA
WHOA!

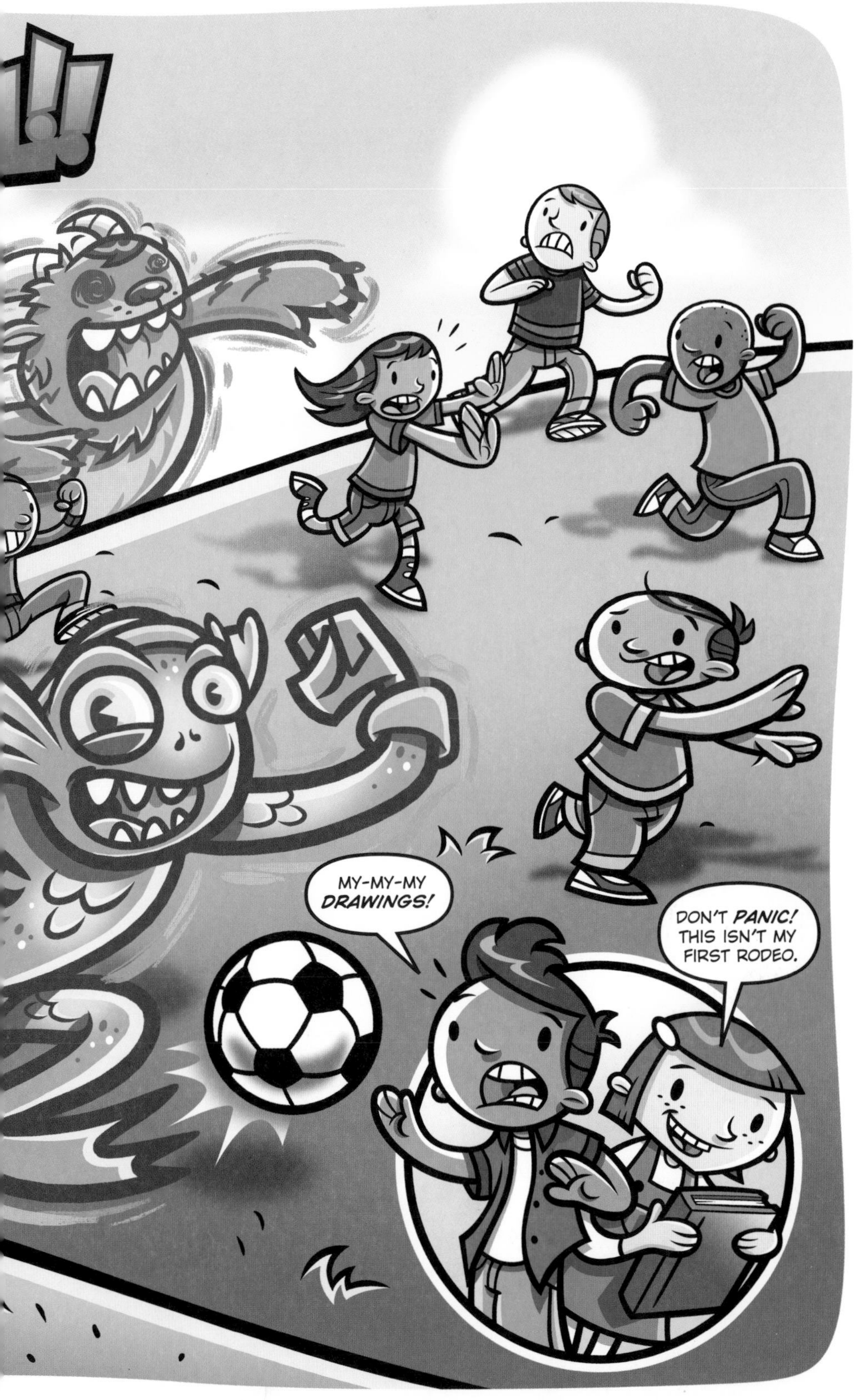
MY-MY-MY *DRAWINGS!*
DON'T *PANIC!* THIS ISN'T MY FIRST RODEO.

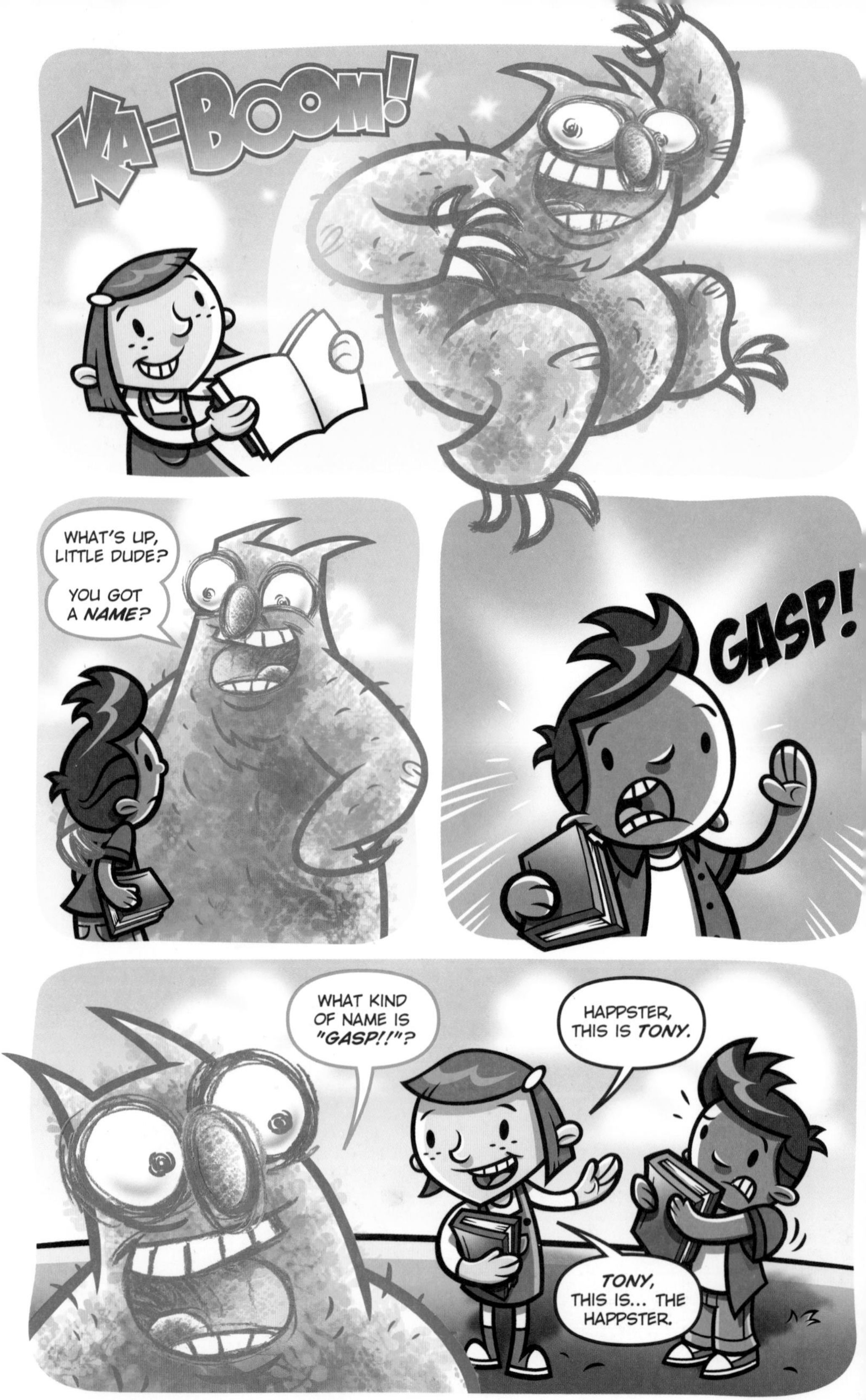
KA-BOOM!
WHAT'S UP, LITTLE DUDE?
YOU GOT A *NAME?*
GASP!
WHAT KIND OF NAME IS *"GASP!!"*?
HAPPSTER, THIS IS *TONY.*
TONY, THIS IS... THE HAPPSTER.

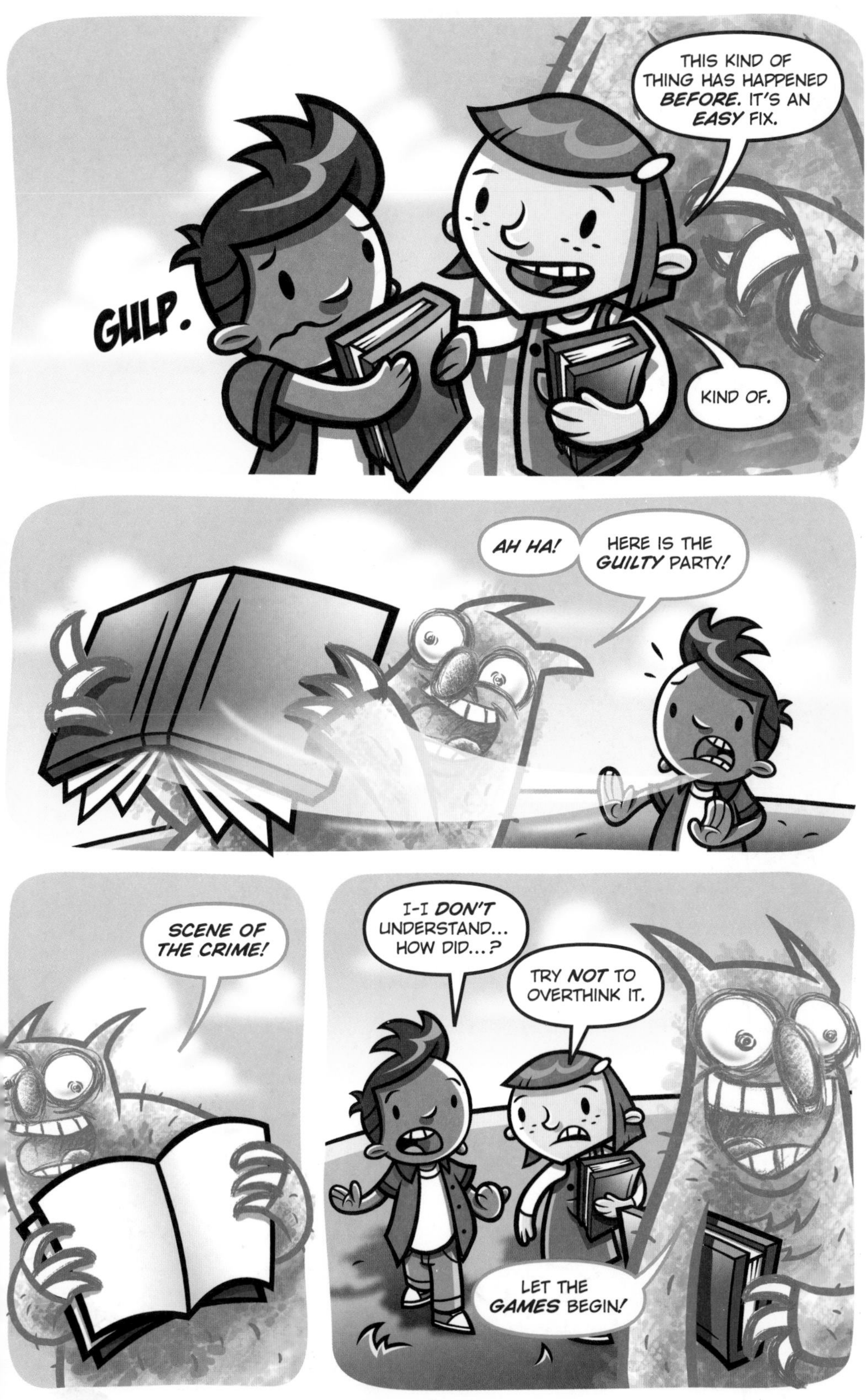
THIS KIND OF THING HAS HAPPENED BEFORE. IT'S AN EASY FIX.
GULP.
KIND OF.
AH HA!
HERE IS THE GUILTY PARTY!
SCENE OF THE CRIME!
I-I DON'T UNDERSTAND... HOW DID...?
TRY NOT TO OVERTHINK IT.
LET THE GAMES BEGIN!

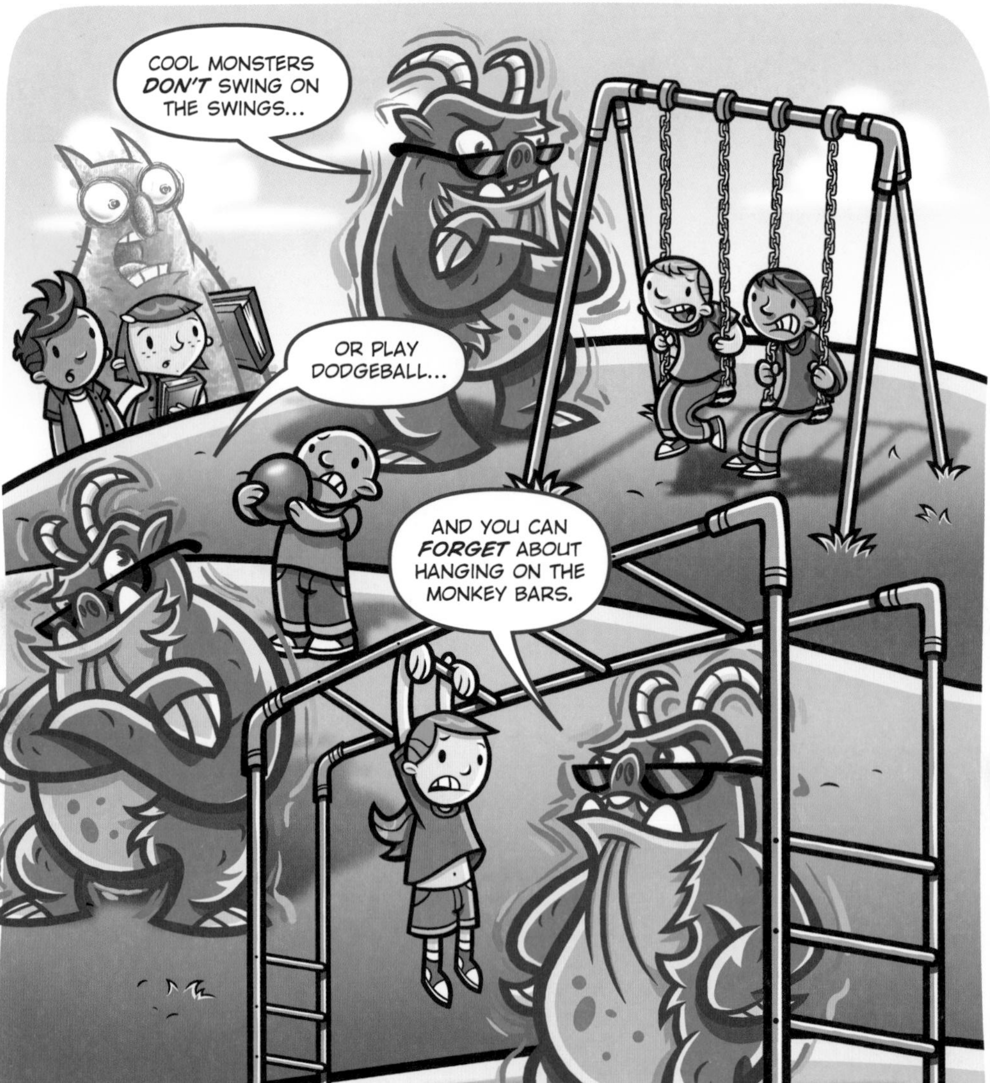
COOL MONSTERS
DON'T SWING ON
THE SWINGS...
OR PLAY
DODGEBALL...
AND YOU CAN
FORGET ABOUT
HANGING ON THE
MONKEY BARS.

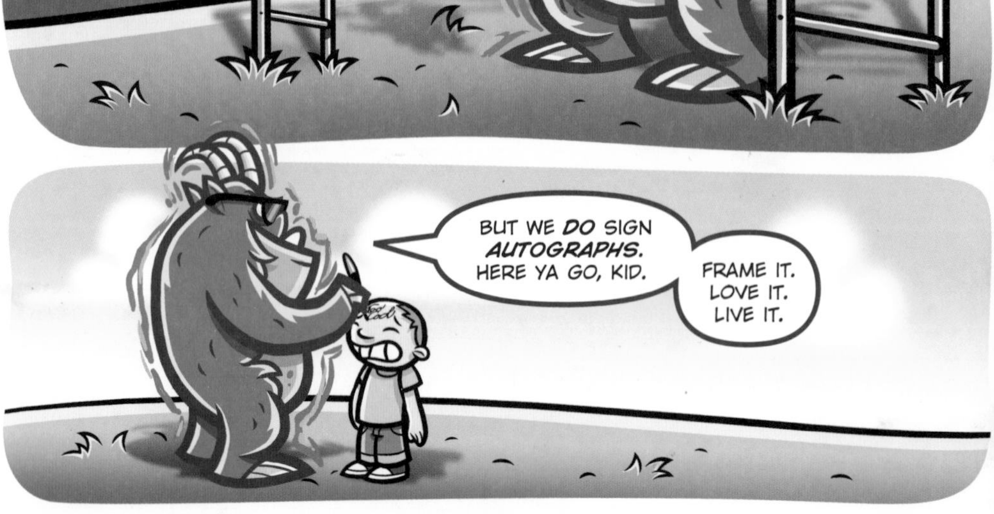
BUT WE DO SIGN
AUTOGRAPHS.
HERE YA GO, KID.
FRAME IT.
LOVE IT.
LIVE IT.

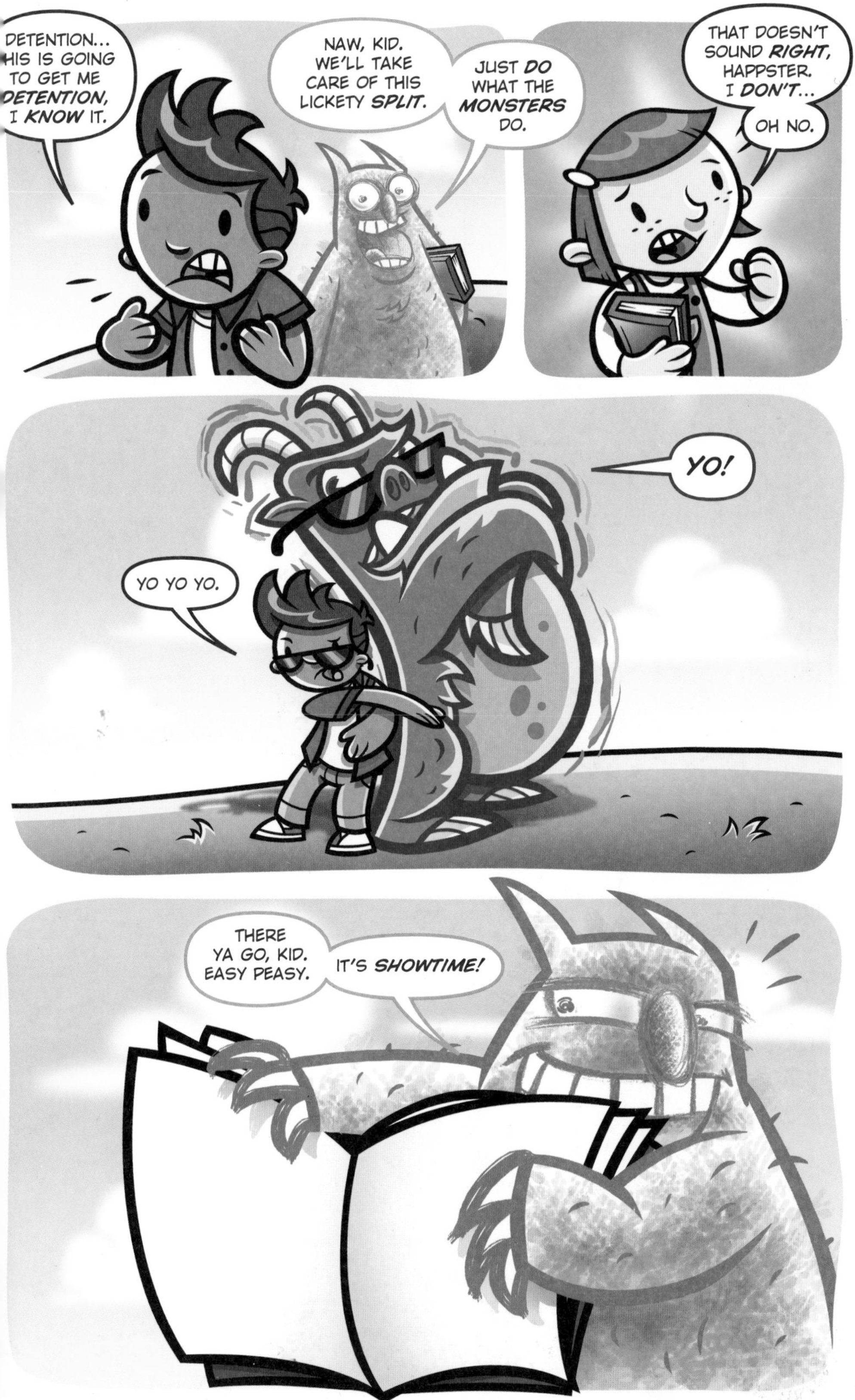
DETENTION... HIS IS GOING TO GET ME DETENTION, I KNOW IT.
NAW, KID. WE'LL TAKE CARE OF THIS LICKETY SPLIT.
JUST DO WHAT THE MONSTERS DO.
THAT DOESN'T SOUND RIGHT, HAPPSTER. I DON'T...
OH NO.
YO!
YO YO YO.
THERE YA GO, KID. EASY PEASY.
IT'S SHOWTIME!

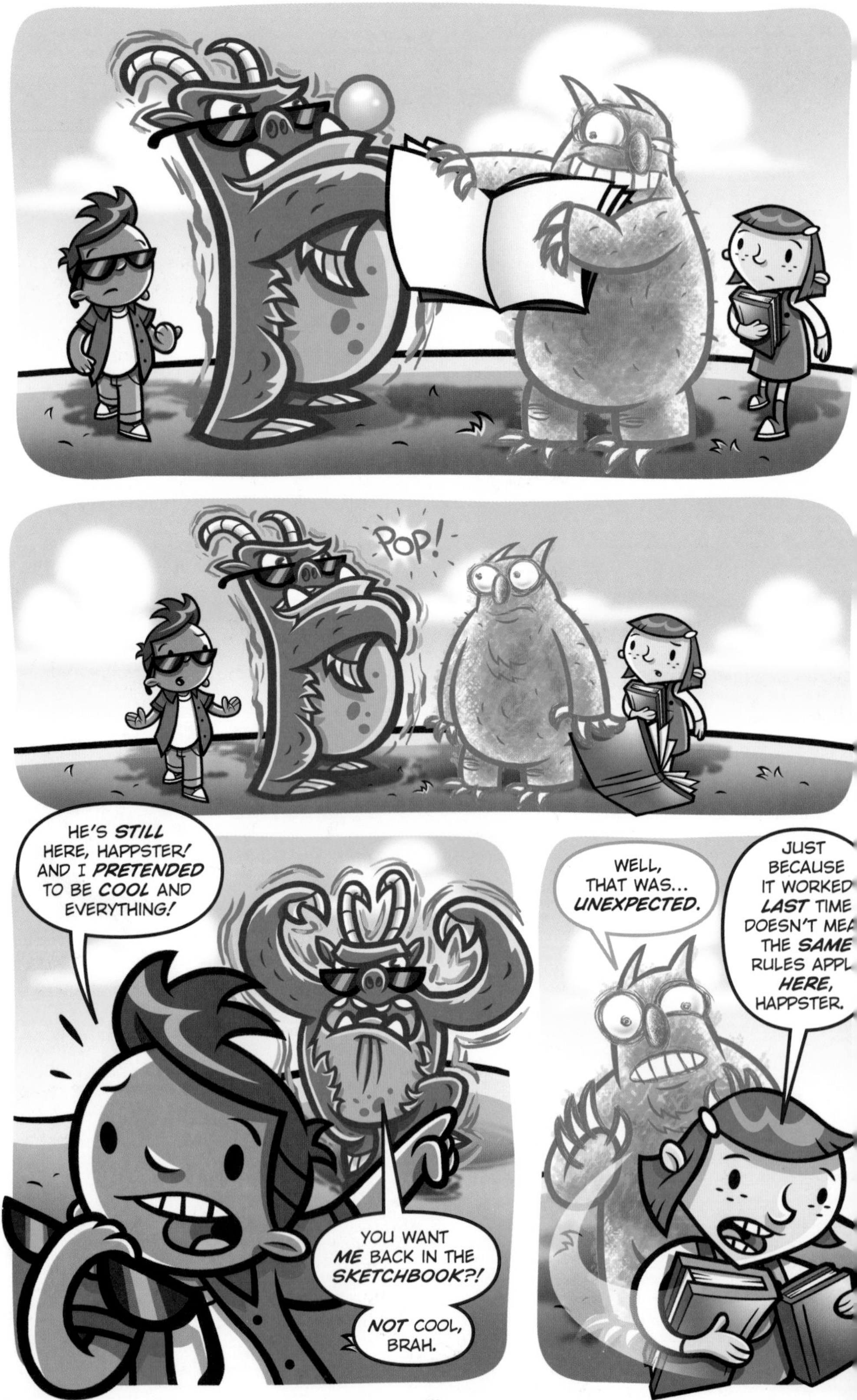

POP!
HE'S STILL HERE, HAPPSTER! AND I PRETENDED TO BE COOL AND EVERYTHING!
YOU WANT ME BACK IN THE SKETCHBOOK?!
NOT COOL, BRAH.
WELL, THAT WAS... UNEXPECTED.
JUST BECAUSE IT WORKED LAST TIME DOESN'T MEA THE SAME RULES APPL HERE, HAPPSTER.

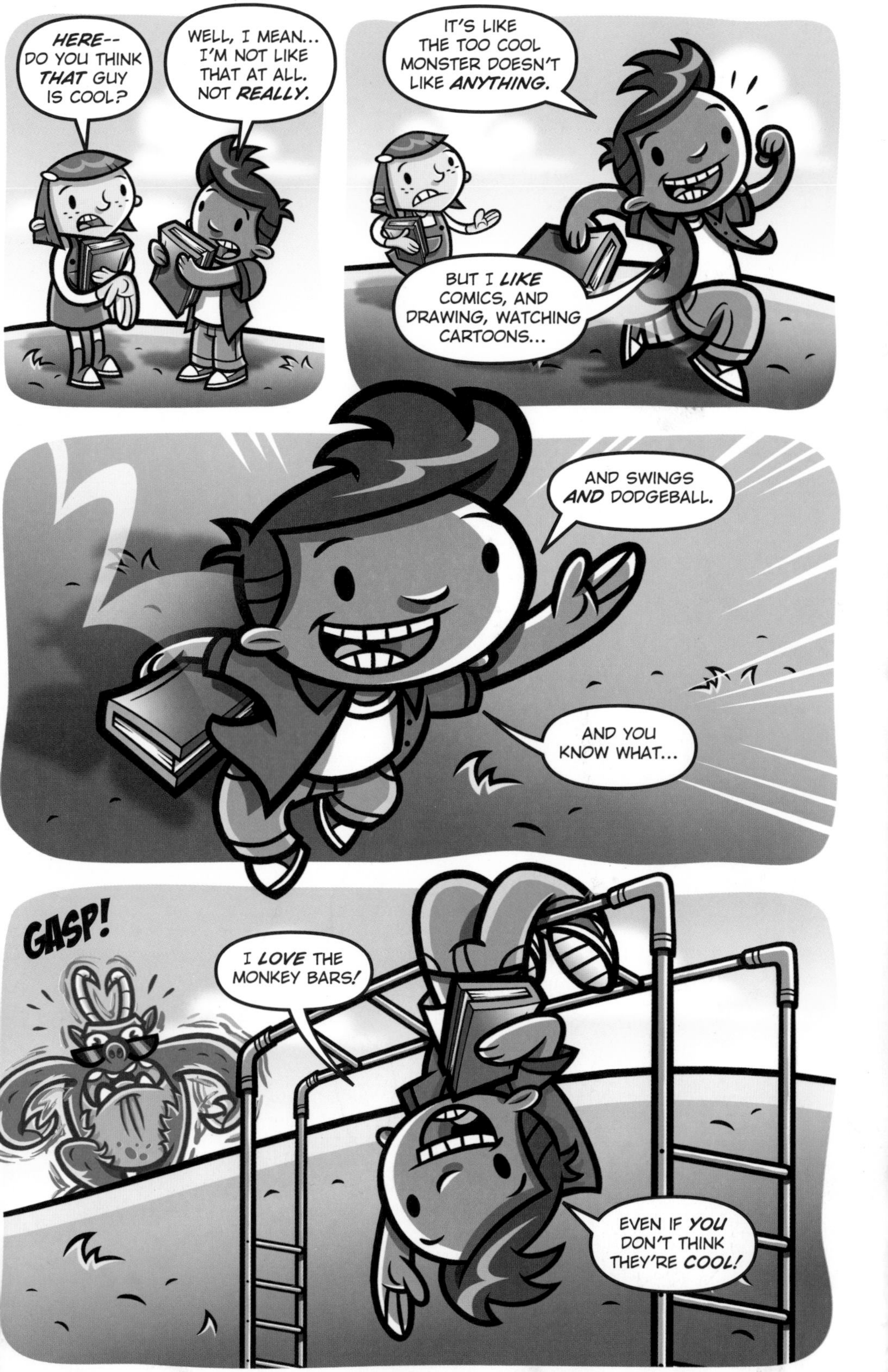
HERE-- DO YOU THINK THAT GUY IS COOL?
WELL, I MEAN... I'M NOT LIKE THAT AT ALL. NOT REALLY.
IT'S LIKE THE TOO COOL MONSTER DOESN'T LIKE ANYTHING.
BUT I LIKE COMICS, AND DRAWING, WATCHING CARTOONS...
AND SWINGS AND DODGEBALL.
AND YOU KNOW WHAT...
GASP!
I LOVE THE MONKEY BARS!
EVEN IF YOU DON'T THINK THEY'RE COOL!

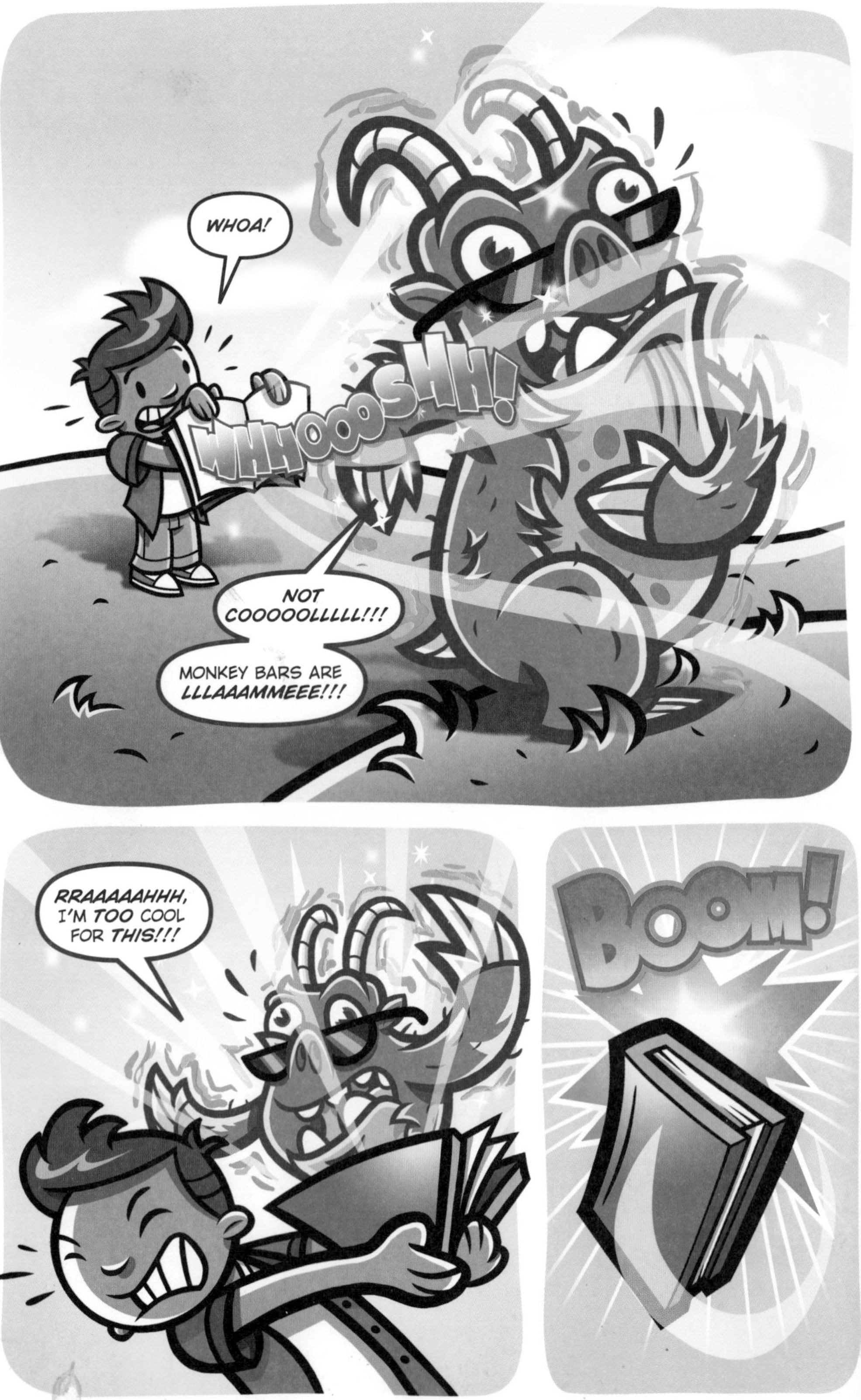
WHOA!
WHHOOOSHH!
NOT COOOOOLLLLLL!!!
MONKEY BARS ARE LLLAAAMMEEE!!!
RRAAAAAHHH, I'M TOO COOL FOR THIS!!!
BOOM!

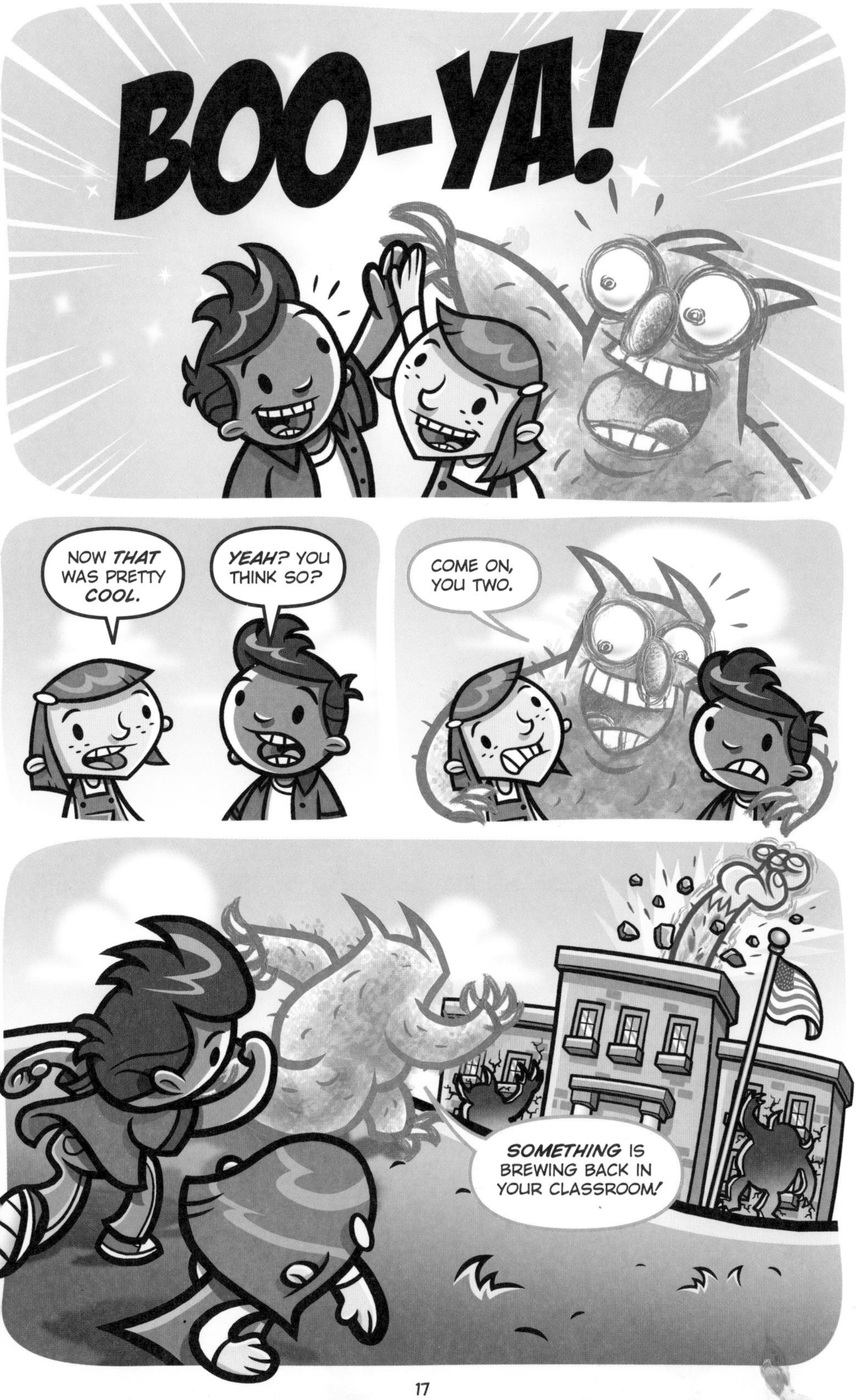
BOO-YA!
NOW THAT WAS PRETTY COOL.
YEAH? YOU THINK SO?
COME ON, YOU TWO.
SOMETHING IS BREWING BACK IN YOUR CLASSROOM!

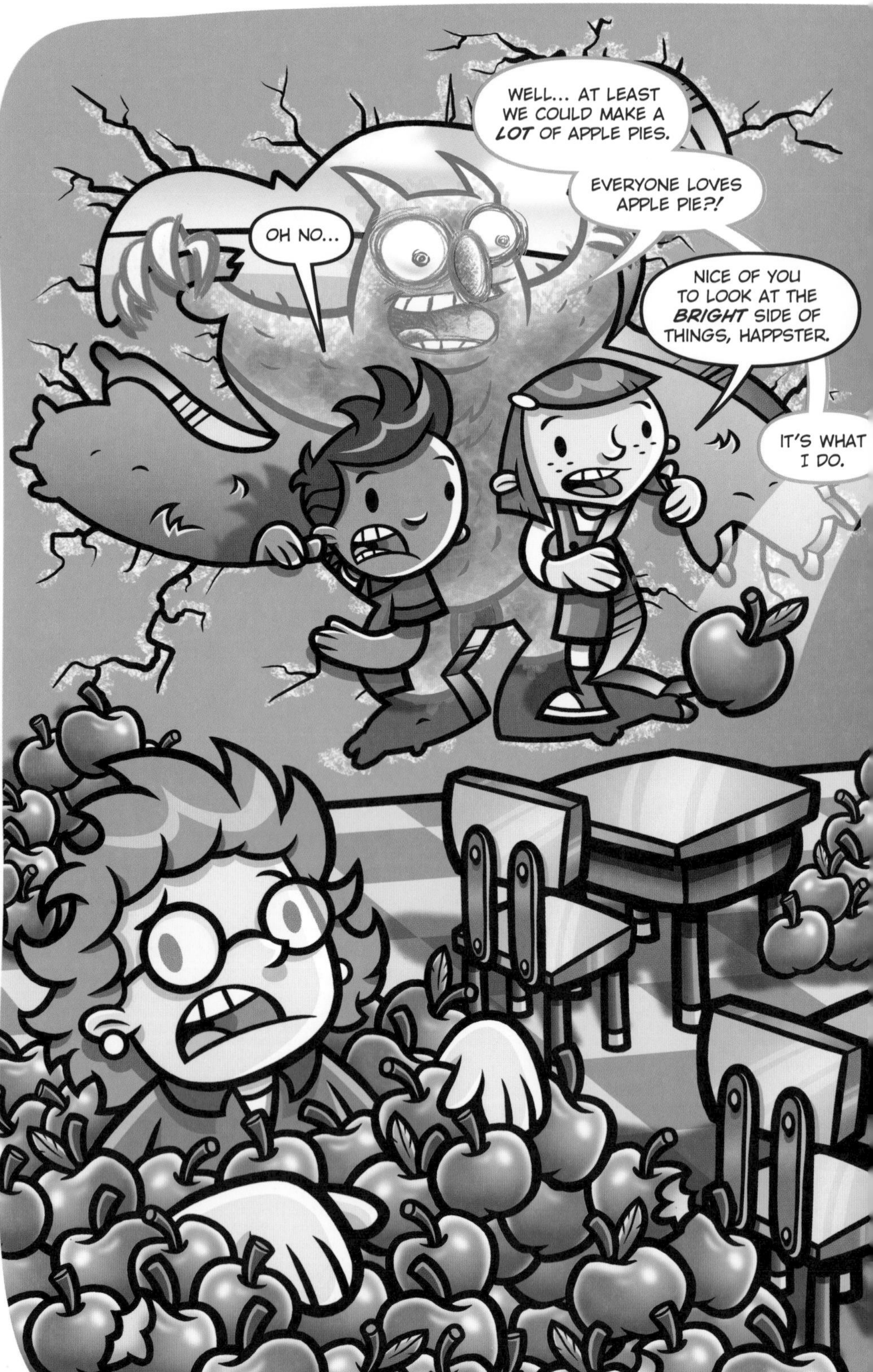
OH NO...
WELL... AT LEAST WE COULD MAKE A *LOT* OF APPLE PIES.
EVERYONE LOVES APPLE PIE?!
NICE OF YOU TO LOOK AT THE *BRIGHT* SIDE OF THINGS, HAPPSTER.
IT'S WHAT I DO.

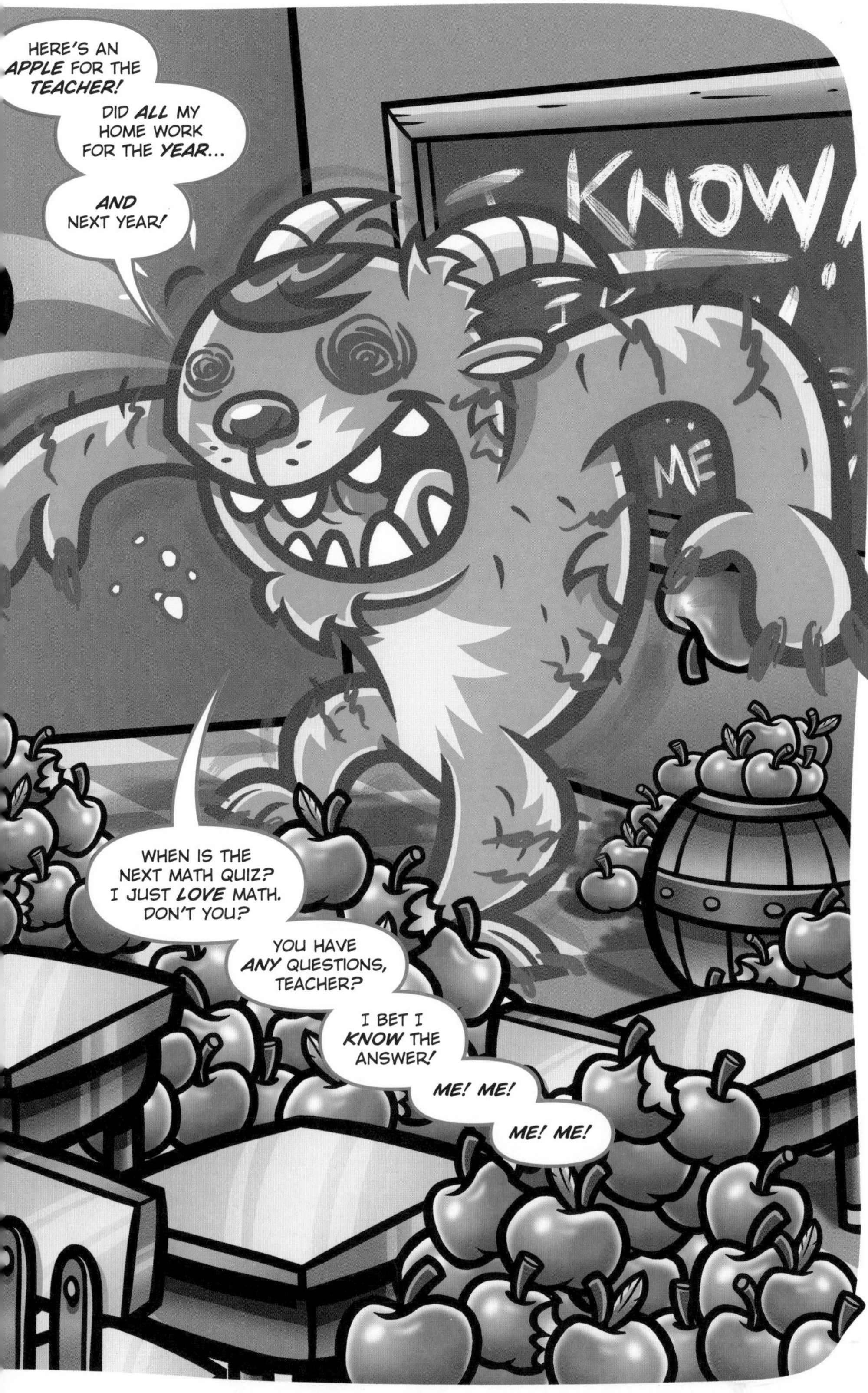
HERE'S AN *APPLE* FOR THE *TEACHER!*
DID *ALL* MY HOME WORK FOR THE *YEAR*...
AND NEXT YEAR!
KNOW
ME
WHEN IS THE NEXT MATH QUIZ? I JUST *LOVE* MATH. DON'T YOU?
YOU HAVE *ANY* QUESTIONS, TEACHER?
I BET I *KNOW* THE ANSWER!
ME! ME!
ME! ME!

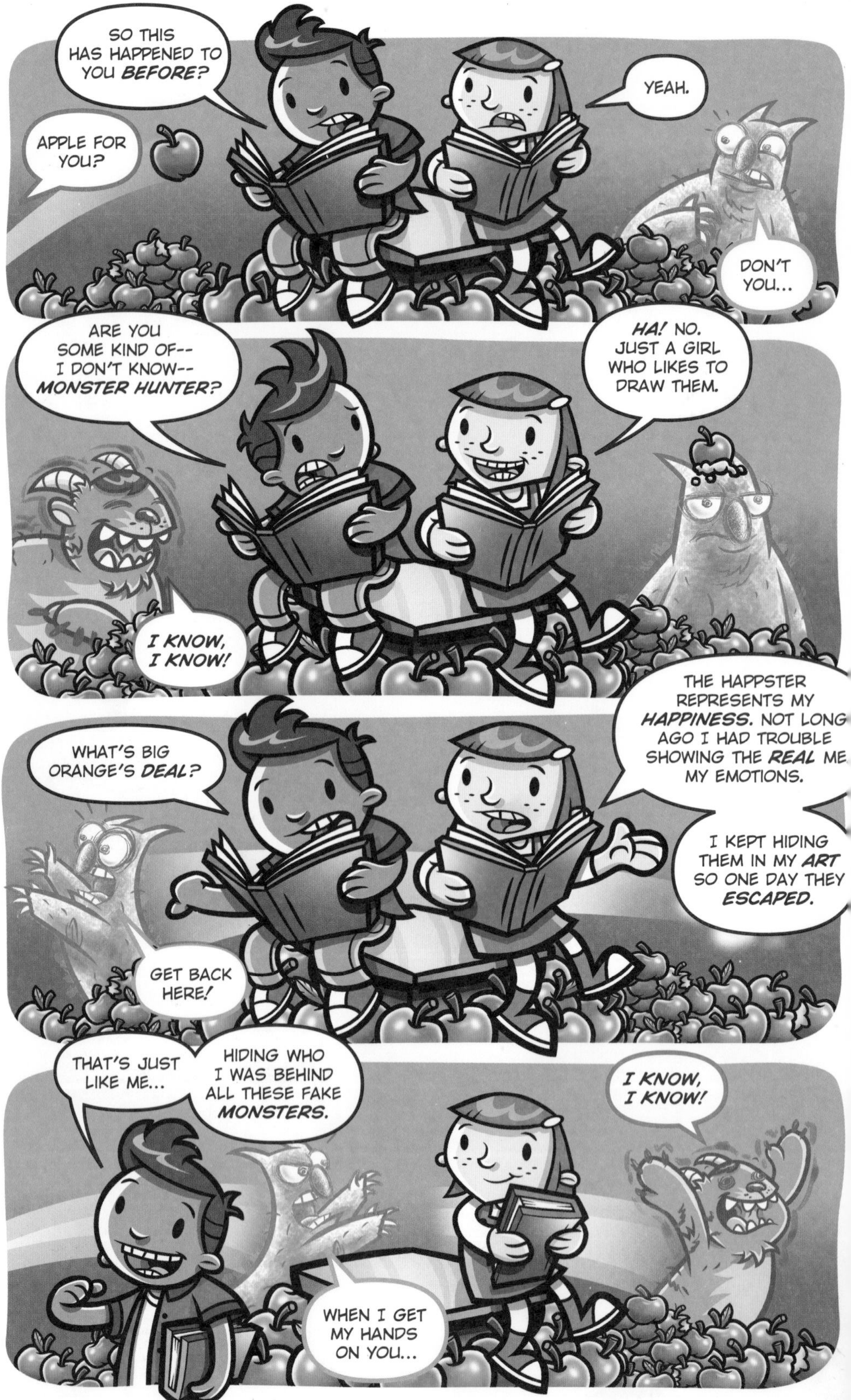
SO THIS HAS HAPPENED TO YOU *BEFORE?*
YEAH.
APPLE FOR YOU?
DON'T YOU...
ARE YOU SOME KIND OF-- I DON'T KNOW-- ***MONSTER HUNTER?***
HA! NO. JUST A GIRL WHO LIKES TO DRAW THEM.
I KNOW, I KNOW!
WHAT'S BIG ORANGE'S ***DEAL?***
THE HAPPSTER REPRESENTS MY ***HAPPINESS.*** NOT LONG AGO I HAD TROUBLE SHOWING THE ***REAL*** ME MY EMOTIONS.
I KEPT HIDING THEM IN MY ***ART*** SO ONE DAY THEY ***ESCAPED.***
GET BACK HERE!
THAT'S JUST LIKE ME...
HIDING WHO I WAS BEHIND ALL THESE FAKE ***MONSTERS.***
I KNOW, I KNOW!
WHEN I GET MY HANDS ON YOU...

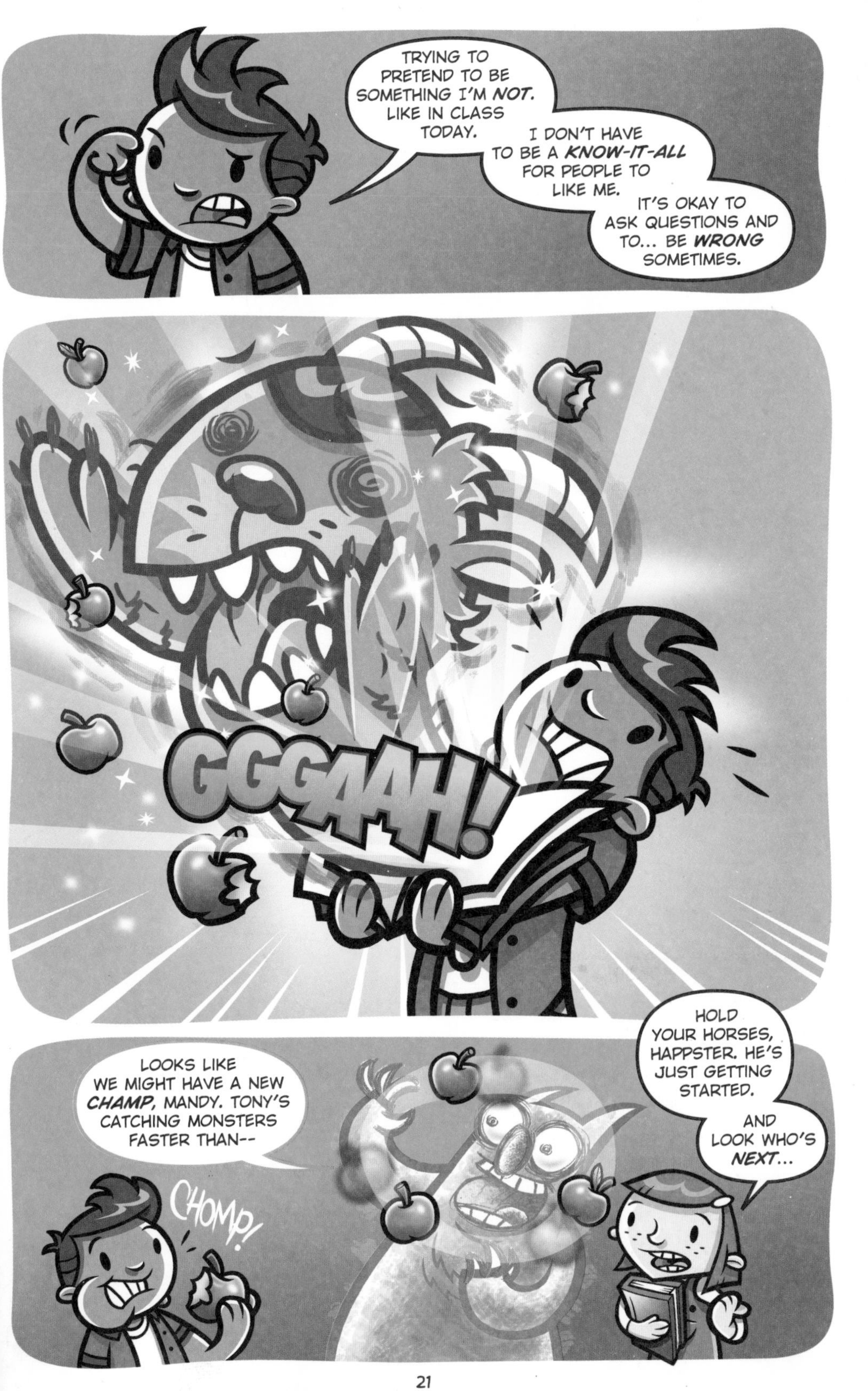

TRYING TO PRETEND TO BE SOMETHING I'M *NOT.* LIKE IN CLASS TODAY.
I DON'T HAVE TO BE A *KNOW-IT-ALL* FOR PEOPLE TO LIKE ME.
IT'S OKAY TO ASK QUESTIONS AND TO... BE *WRONG* SOMETIMES.
GGGAAAH!
LOOKS LIKE WE MIGHT HAVE A NEW *CHAMP,* MANDY. TONY'S CATCHING MONSTERS FASTER THAN--
CHOMP!
HOLD YOUR HORSES, HAPPSTER. HE'S JUST GETTING STARTED.
AND LOOK WHO'S *NEXT*...

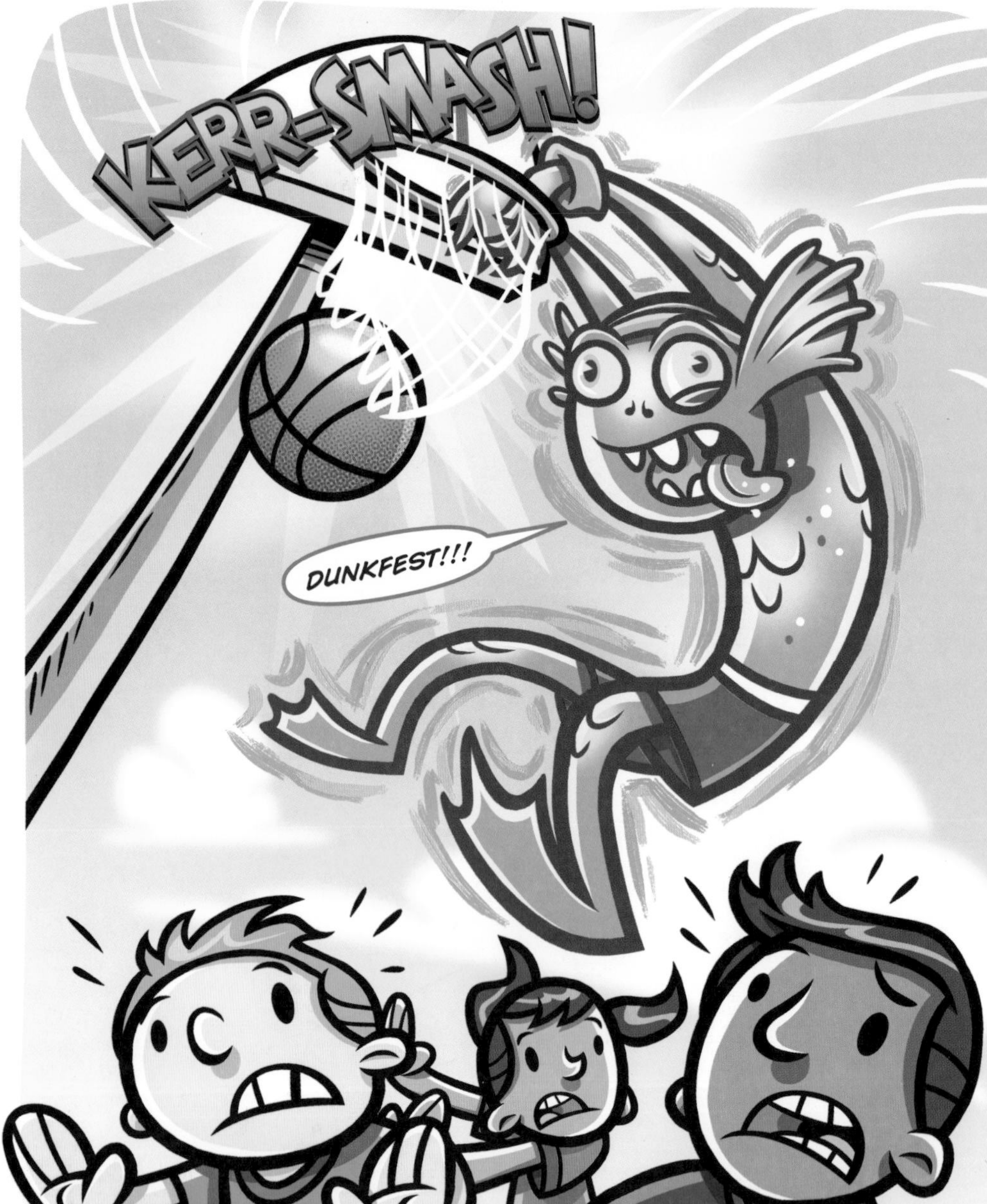
KERR-SMASH!
DUNKFEST!!!

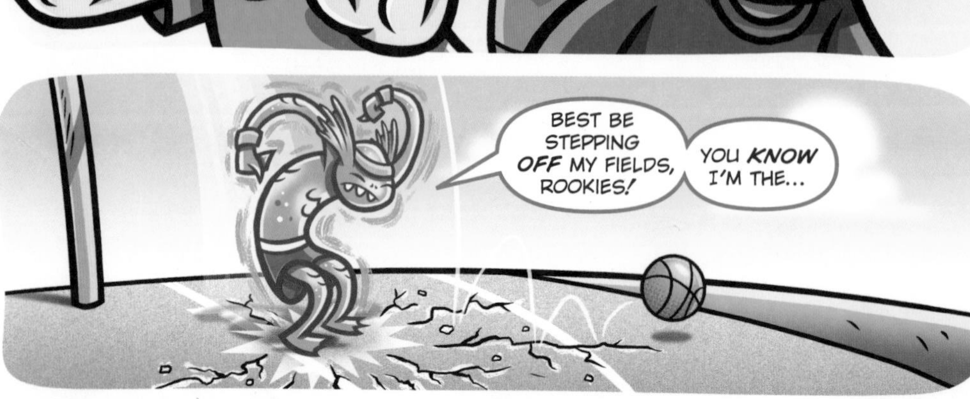
BEST BE STEPPING OFF MY FIELDS, ROOKIES!
YOU KNOW I'M THE...

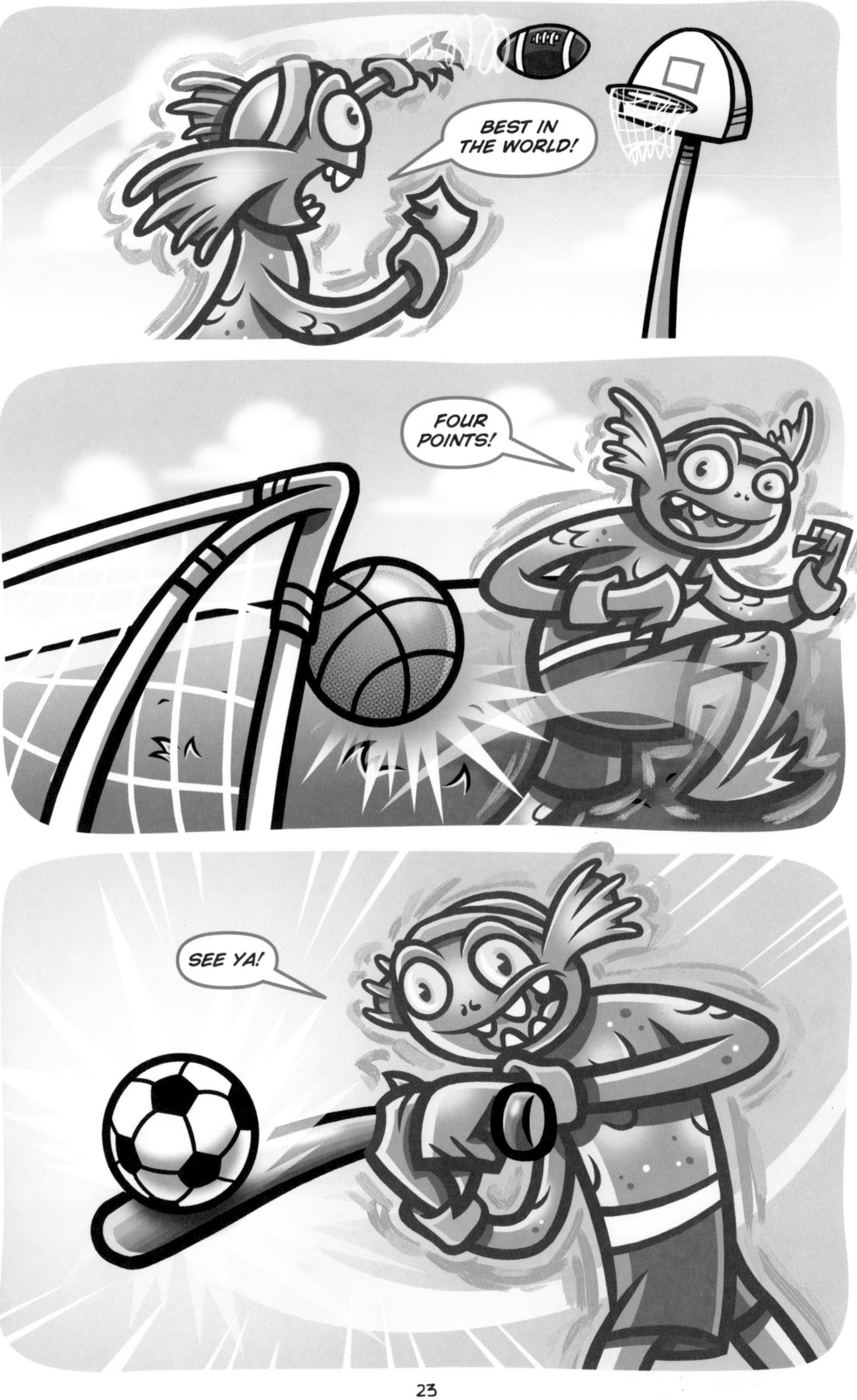
BEST IN THE WORLD!
FOUR POINTS!
SEE YA!

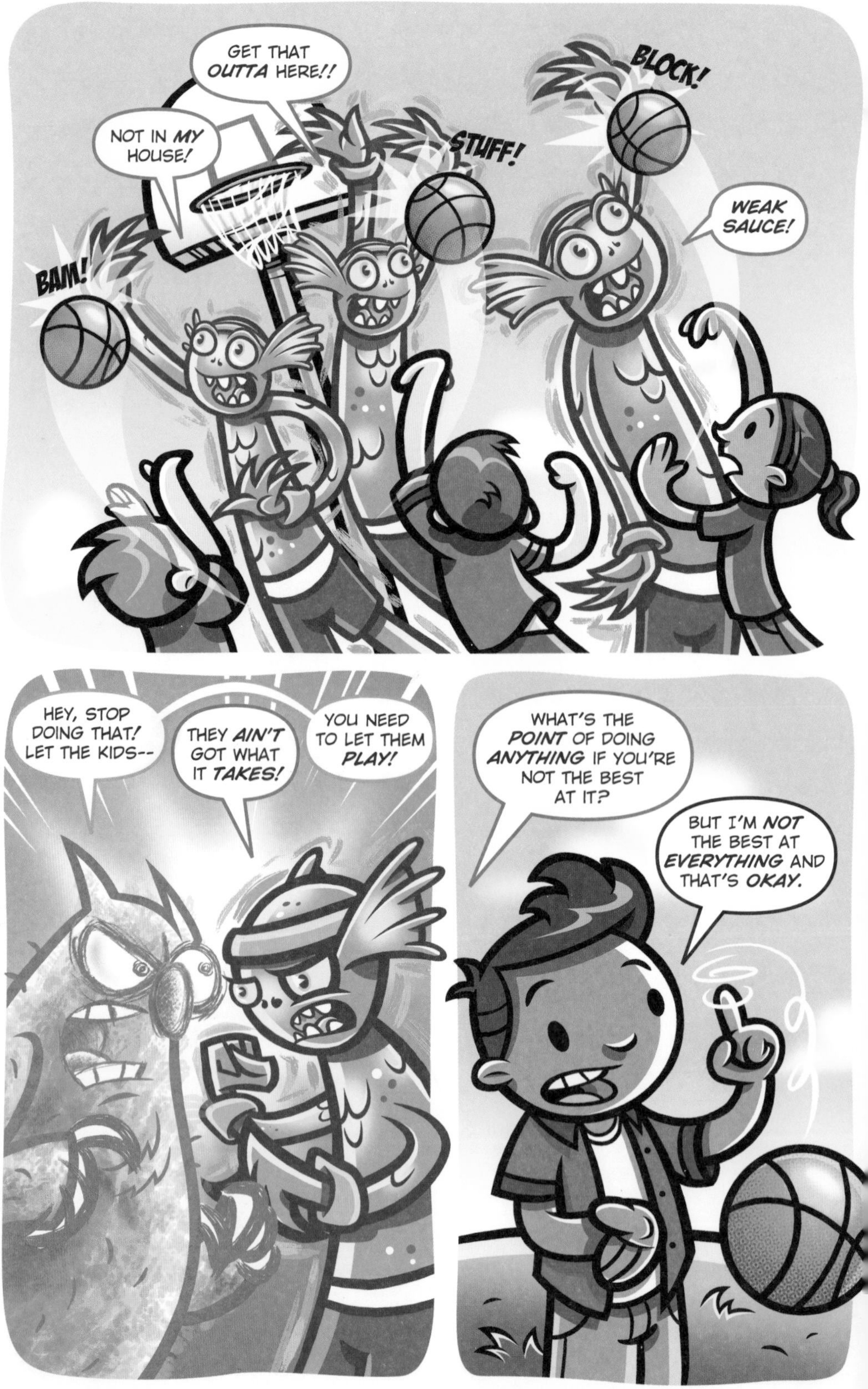
NOT IN MY HOUSE!
GET THAT OUTTA HERE!!
BAM!
STUFF!
BLOCK!
WEAK SAUCE!
HEY, STOP DOING THAT! LET THE KIDS--
THEY AIN'T GOT WHAT IT TAKES!
YOU NEED TO LET THEM PLAY!
WHAT'S THE POINT OF DOING ANYTHING IF YOU'RE NOT THE BEST AT IT?
BUT I'M NOT THE BEST AT EVERYTHING AND THAT'S OKAY.

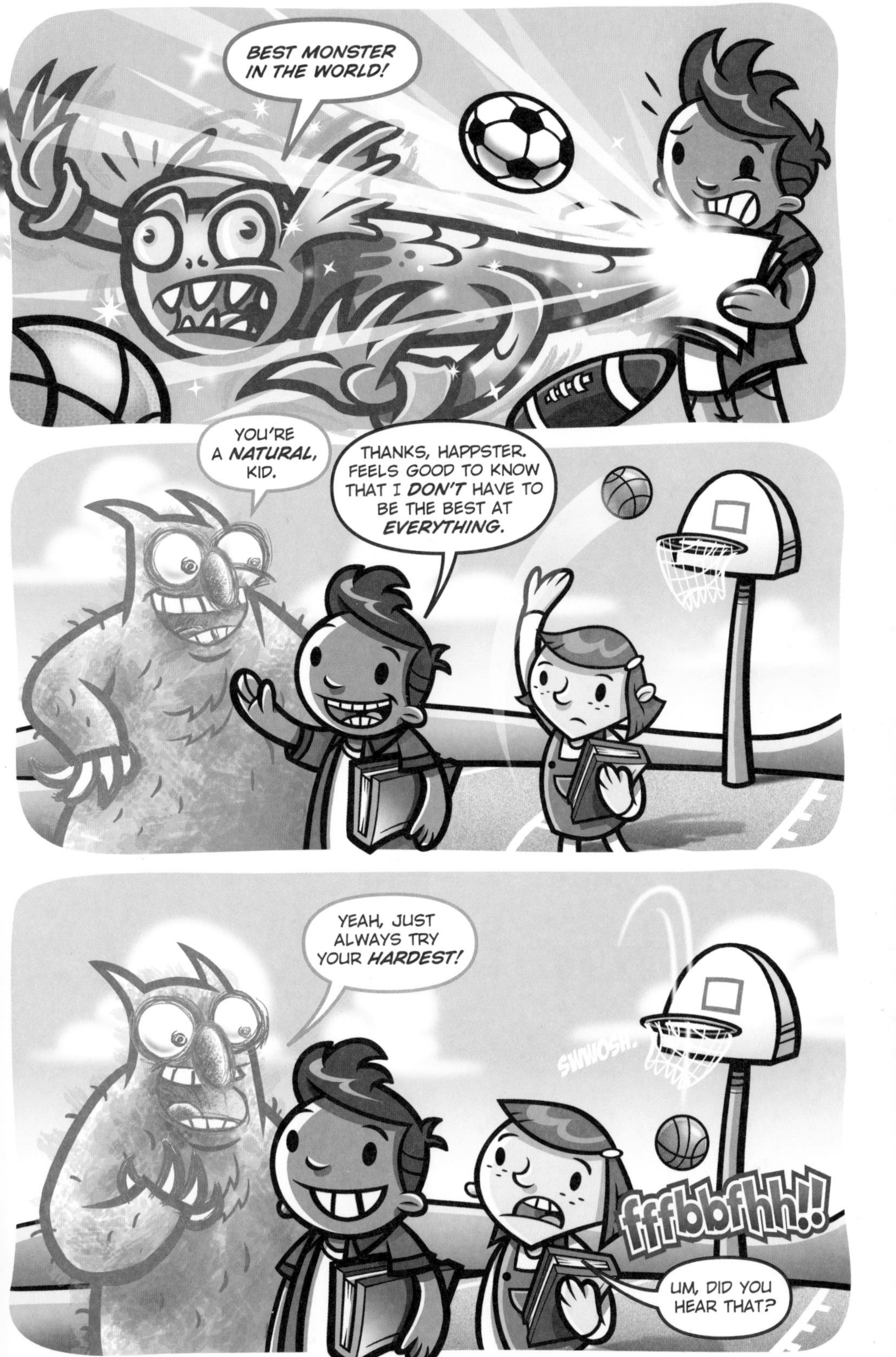
BEST MONSTER IN THE WORLD!
YOU'RE A NATURAL, KID.
THANKS, HAPPSTER. FEELS GOOD TO KNOW THAT I DON'T HAVE TO BE THE BEST AT EVERYTHING.
YEAH, JUST ALWAYS TRY YOUR HARDEST!
SWWOSH.
fffbbfhh!!
UM, DID YOU HEAR THAT?

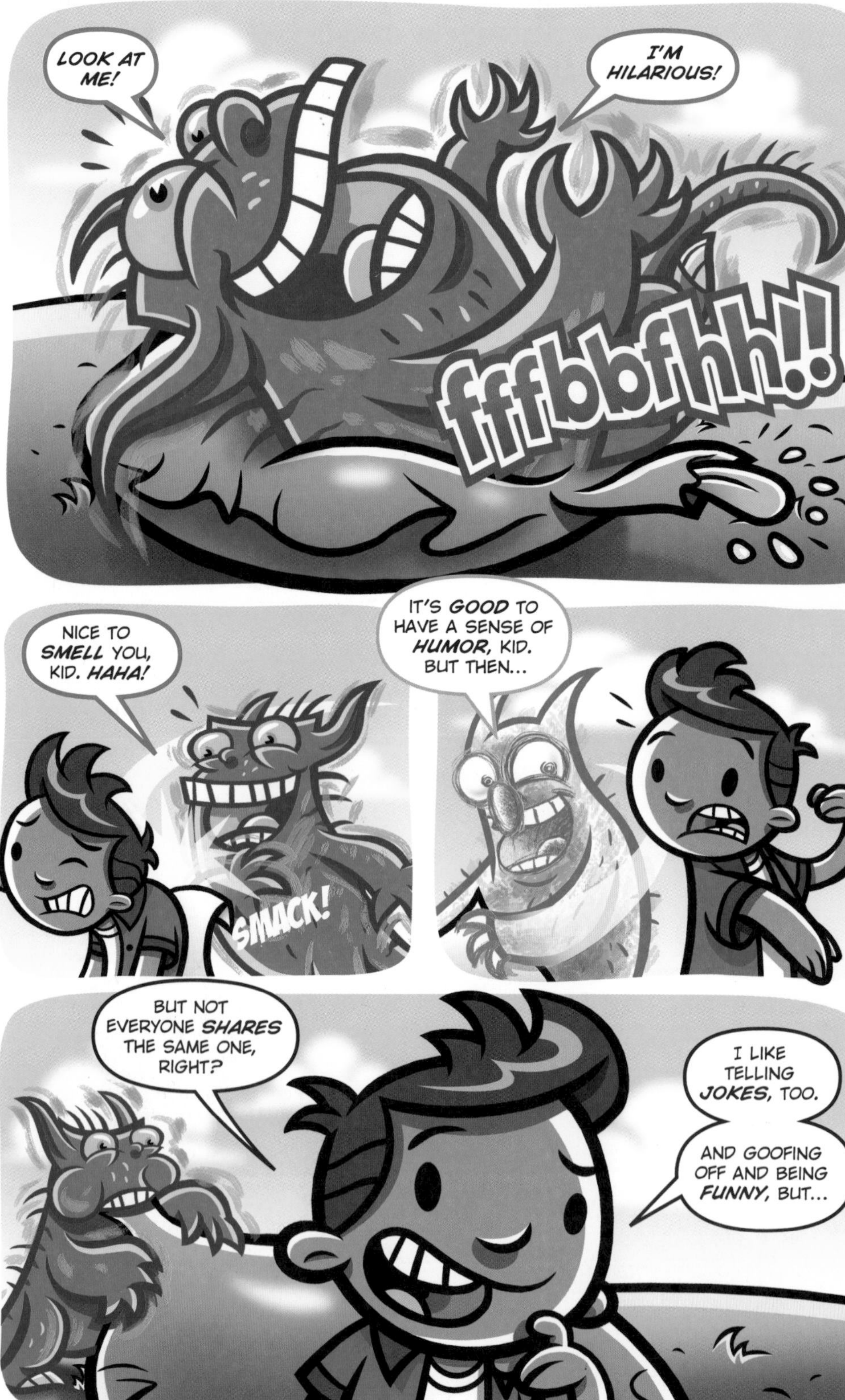

LOOK AT ME!
I'M HILARIOUS!
fffbbfhh!!
NICE TO SMELL YOU, KID. HAHA!
SMACK!
IT'S GOOD TO HAVE A SENSE OF HUMOR, KID. BUT THEN...
BUT NOT EVERYONE SHARES THE SAME ONE, RIGHT?
I LIKE TELLING JOKES, TOO.
AND GOOFING OFF AND BEING FUNNY, BUT...

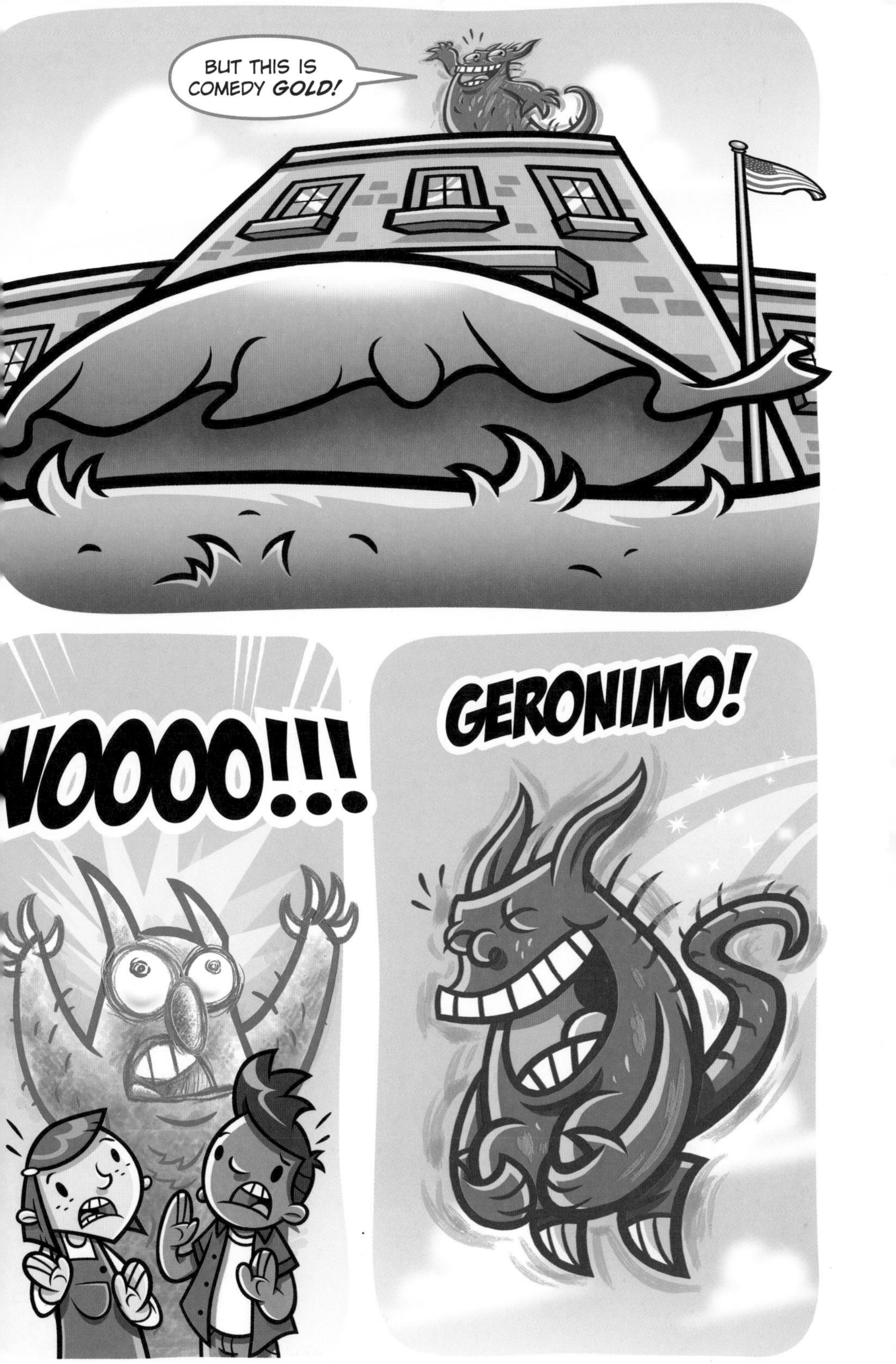
BUT THIS IS COMEDY GOLD!
OOOO!!!
GERONIMO!

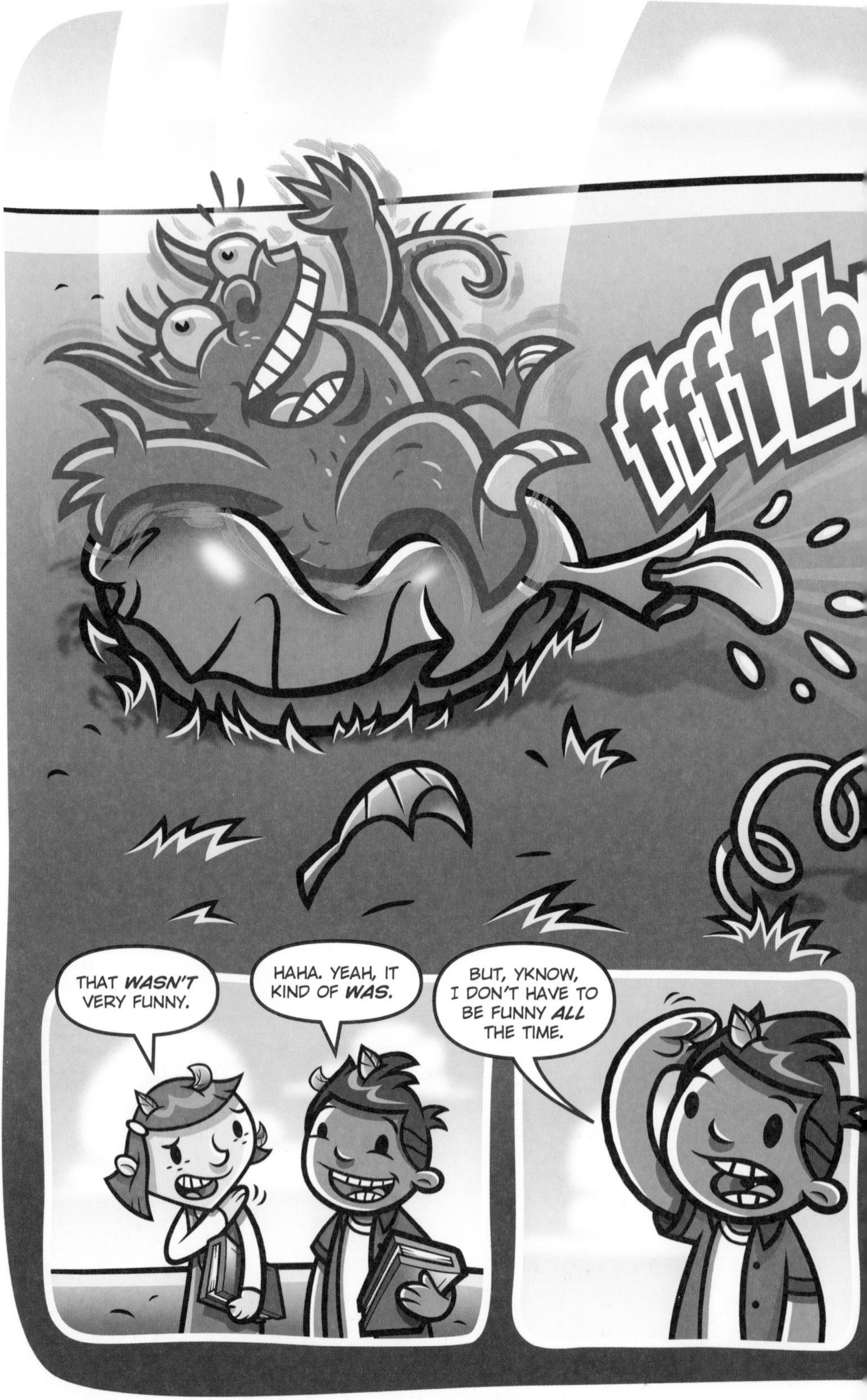
THAT WASN'T VERY FUNNY.
HAHA. YEAH, IT KIND OF WAS.
BUT, YKNOW, I DON'T HAVE TO BE FUNNY ALL THE TIME.

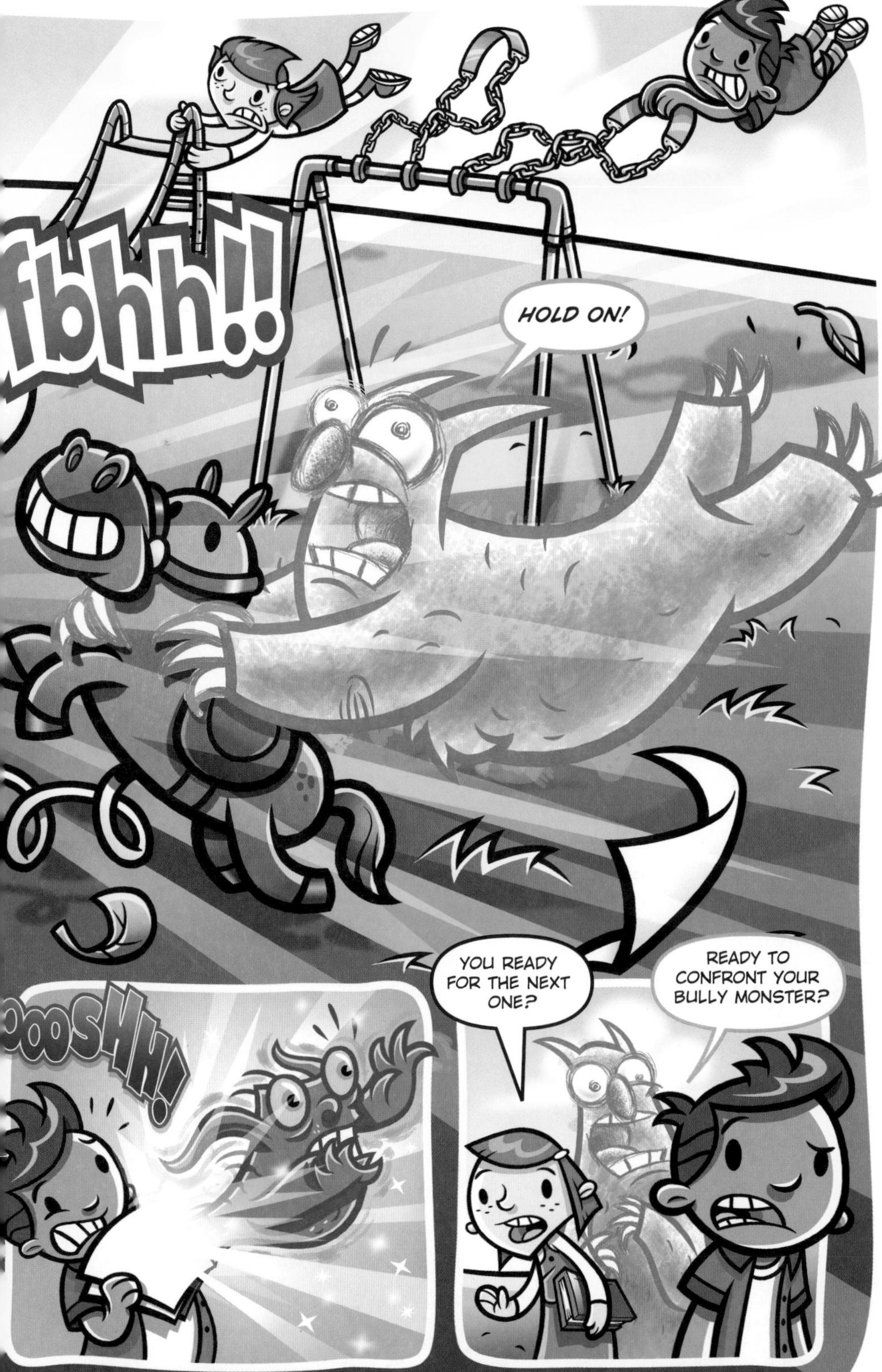
fbhh!!
HOLD ON!
OOOSHH!
YOU READY FOR THE NEXT ONE?
READY TO CONFRONT YOUR BULLY MONSTER?

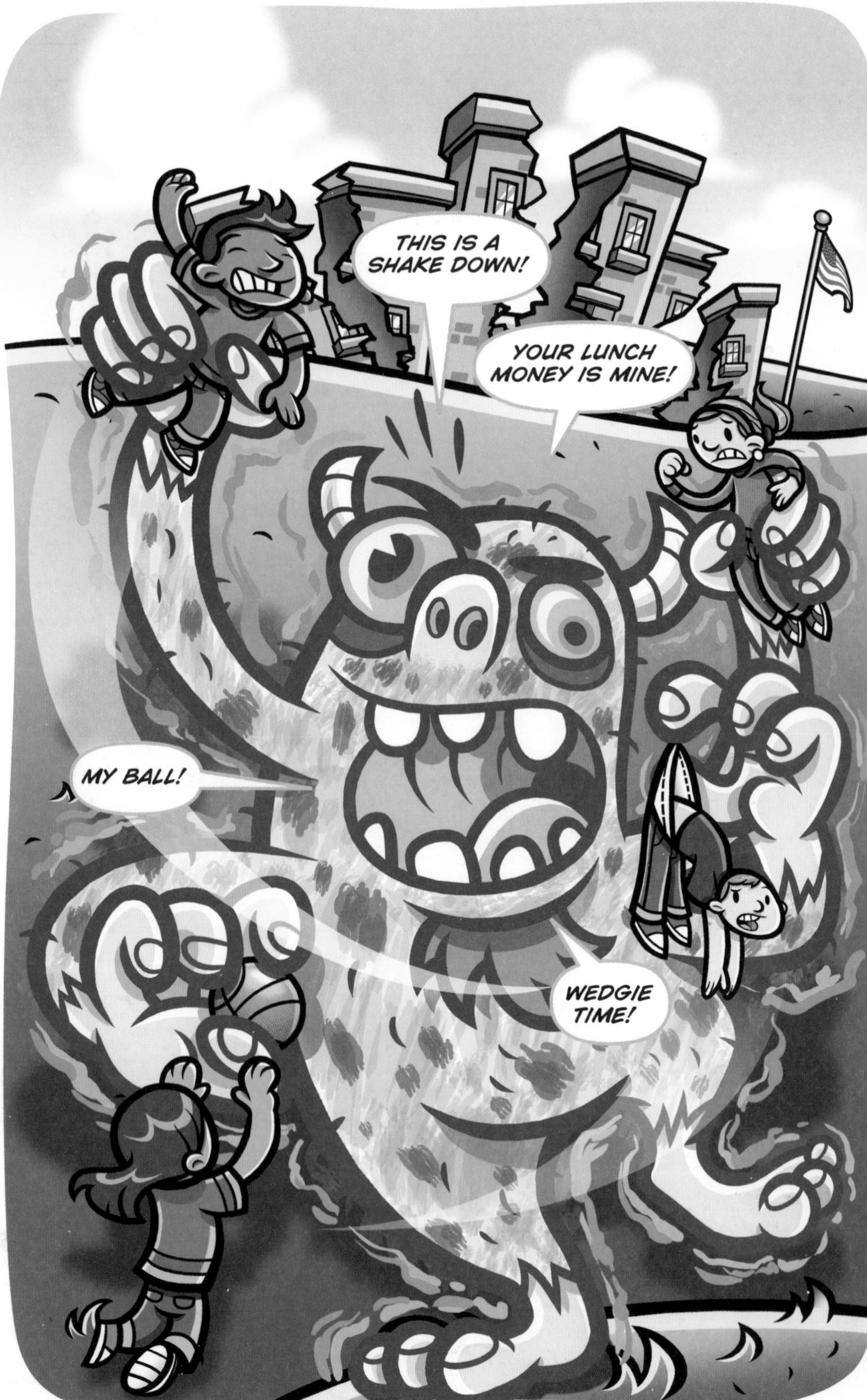
THIS IS A SHAKE DOWN!
YOUR LUNCH MONEY IS MINE!
MY BALL!
WEDGIE TIME!

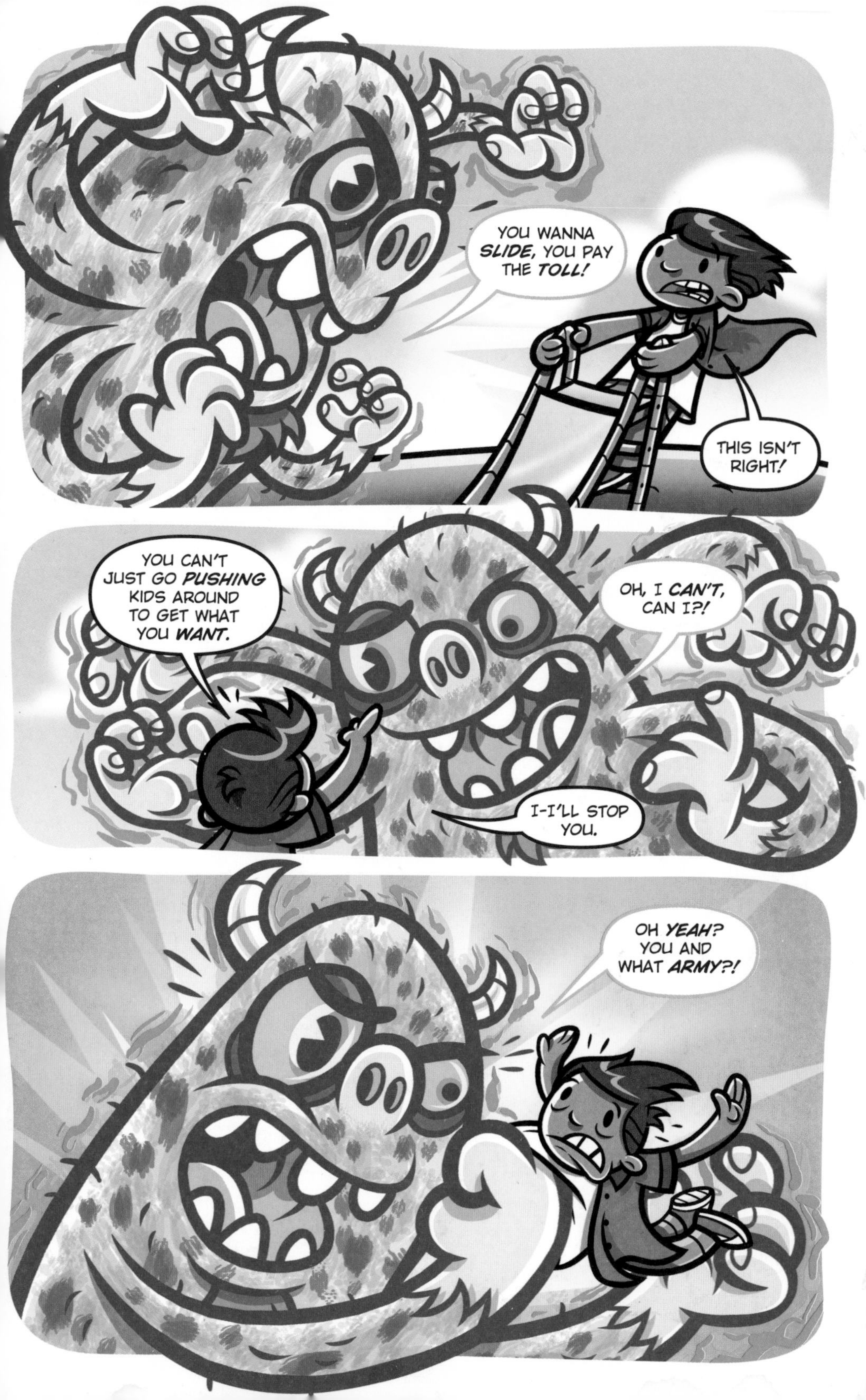
YOU WANNA SLIDE, YOU PAY THE TOLL!
THIS ISN'T RIGHT!
YOU CAN'T JUST GO PUSHING KIDS AROUND TO GET WHAT YOU WANT.
OH, I CAN'T, CAN I?!
I-I'LL STOP YOU.
OH YEAH? YOU AND WHAT ARMY?!

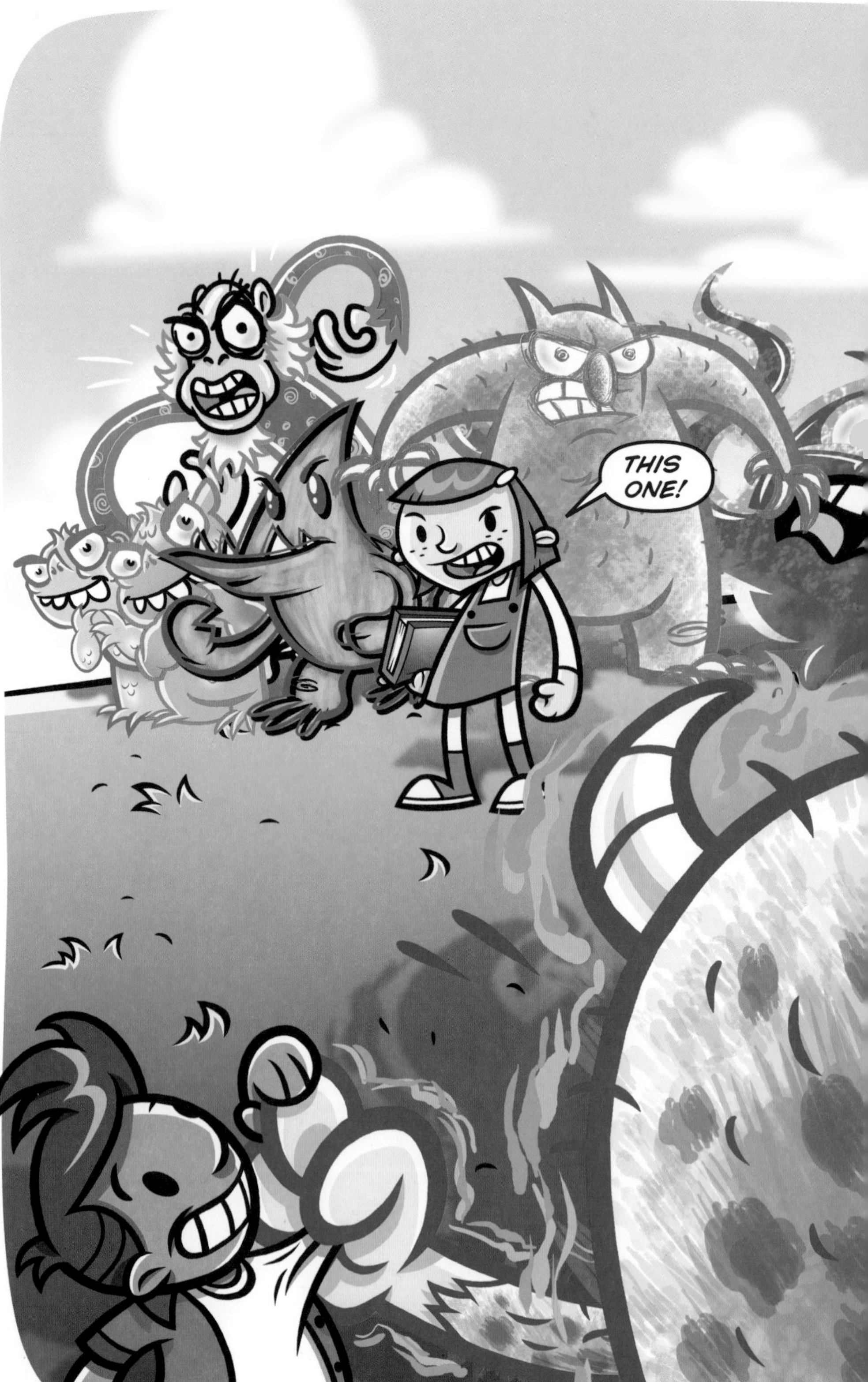
THIS
ONE!

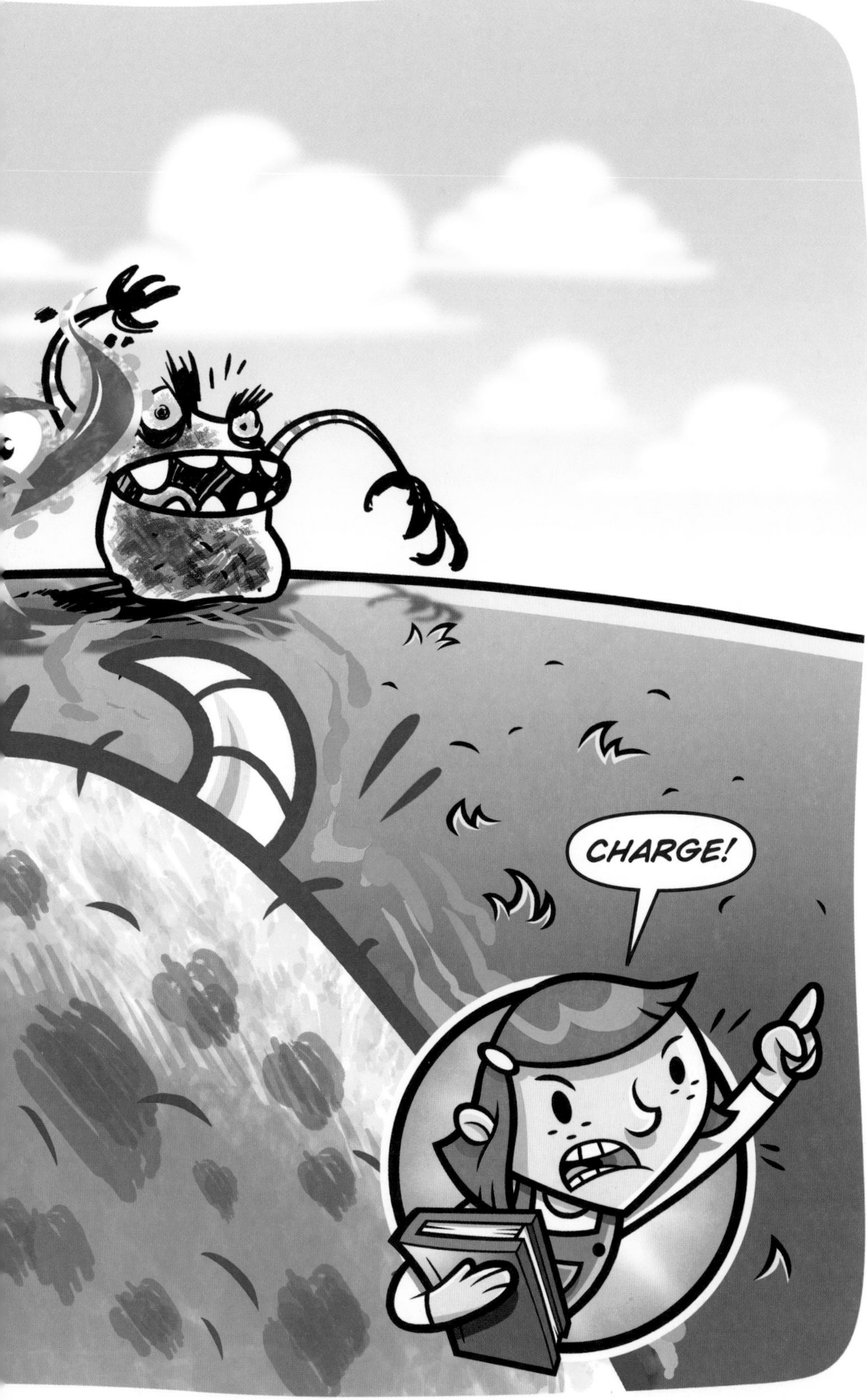
CHARGE!

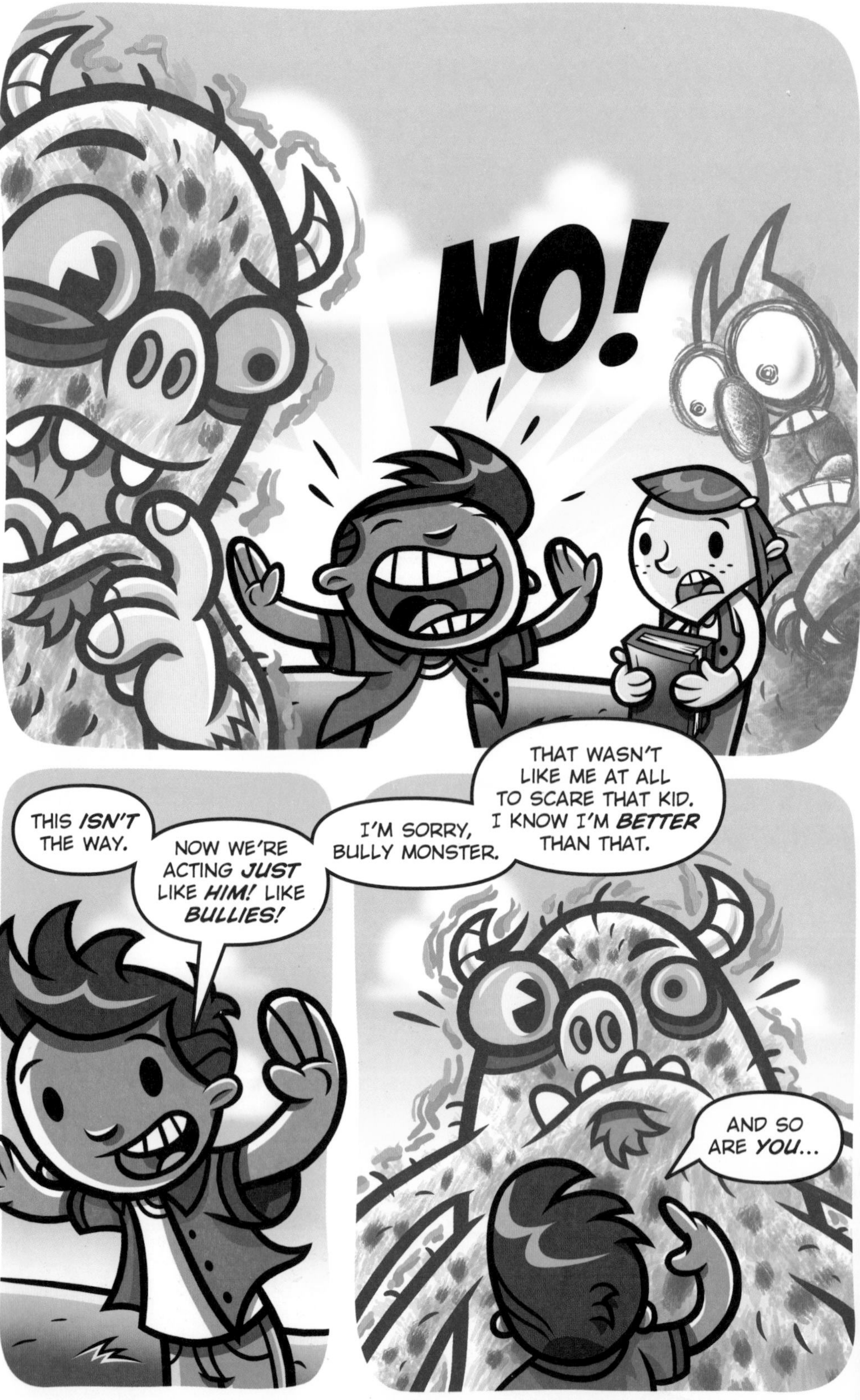
NO!
THIS ISN'T THE WAY.
NOW WE'RE ACTING JUST LIKE HIM! LIKE BULLIES!
I'M SORRY, BULLY MONSTER.
THAT WASN'T LIKE ME AT ALL TO SCARE THAT KID. I KNOW I'M BETTER THAN THAT.
AND SO ARE YOU...

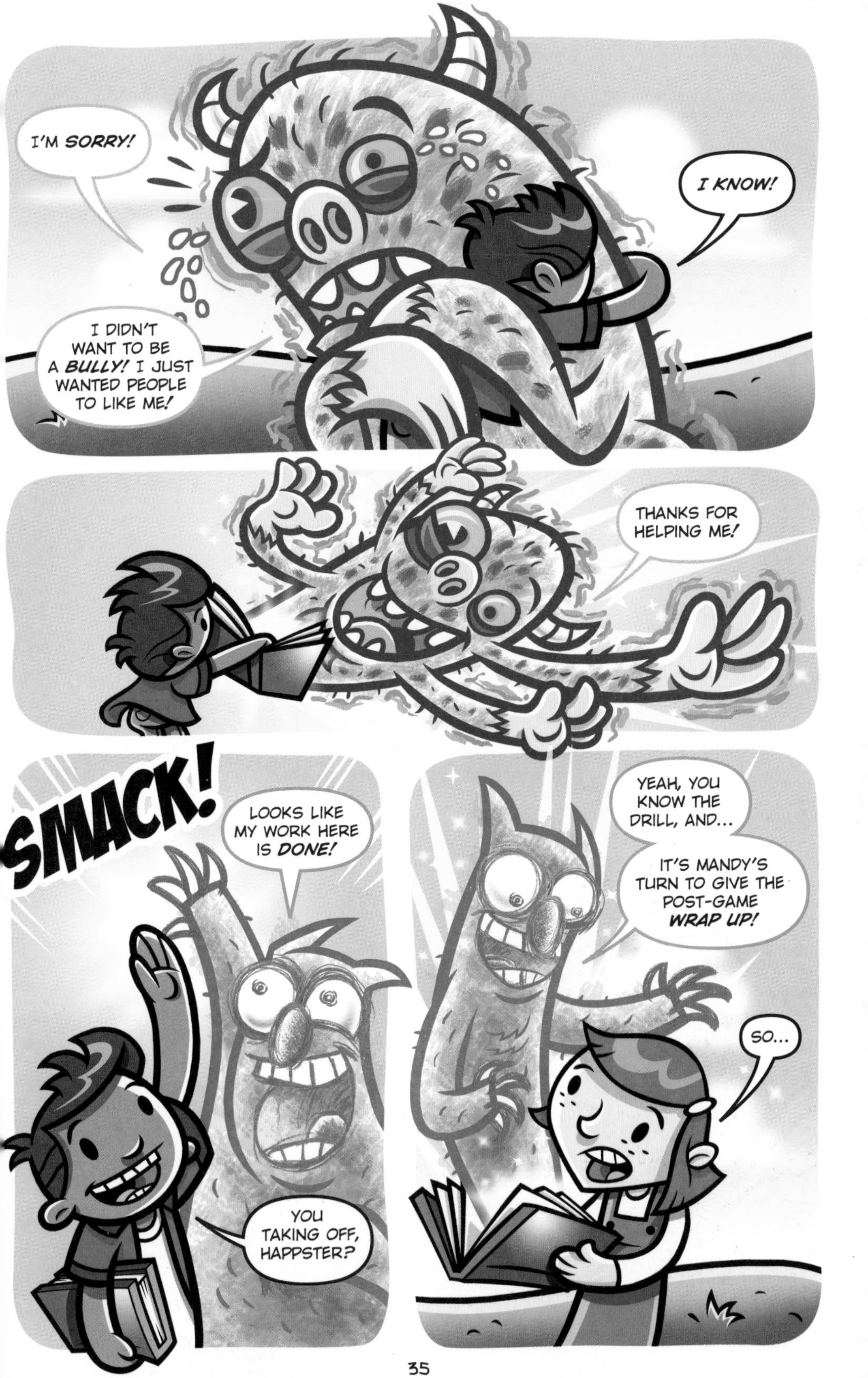
I'M *SORRY!*
I DIDN'T WANT TO BE A *BULLY!* I JUST WANTED PEOPLE TO LIKE ME!
I KNOW!
THANKS FOR HELPING ME!
SMACK!
LOOKS LIKE MY WORK HERE IS *DONE!*
YOU TAKING OFF, HAPPSTER?
YEAH, YOU KNOW THE DRILL, AND...
IT'S MANDY'S TURN TO GIVE THE POST-GAME *WRAP UP!*
SO...

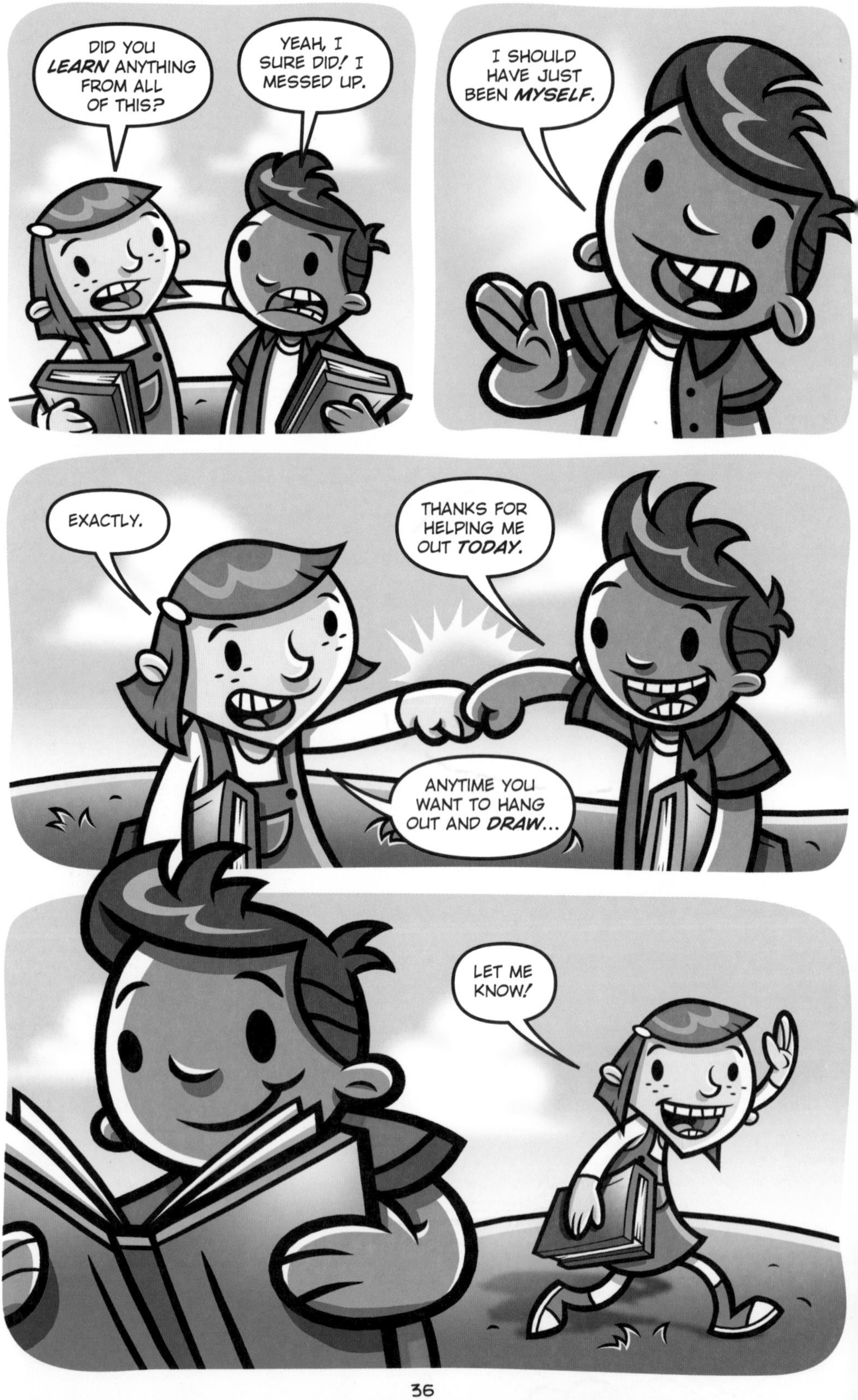
DID YOU LEARN ANYTHING FROM ALL OF THIS?
YEAH, I SURE DID! I MESSED UP.
I SHOULD HAVE JUST BEEN MYSELF.
EXACTLY.
THANKS FOR HELPING ME OUT TODAY.
ANYTIME YOU WANT TO HANG OUT AND DRAW...
LET ME KNOW!

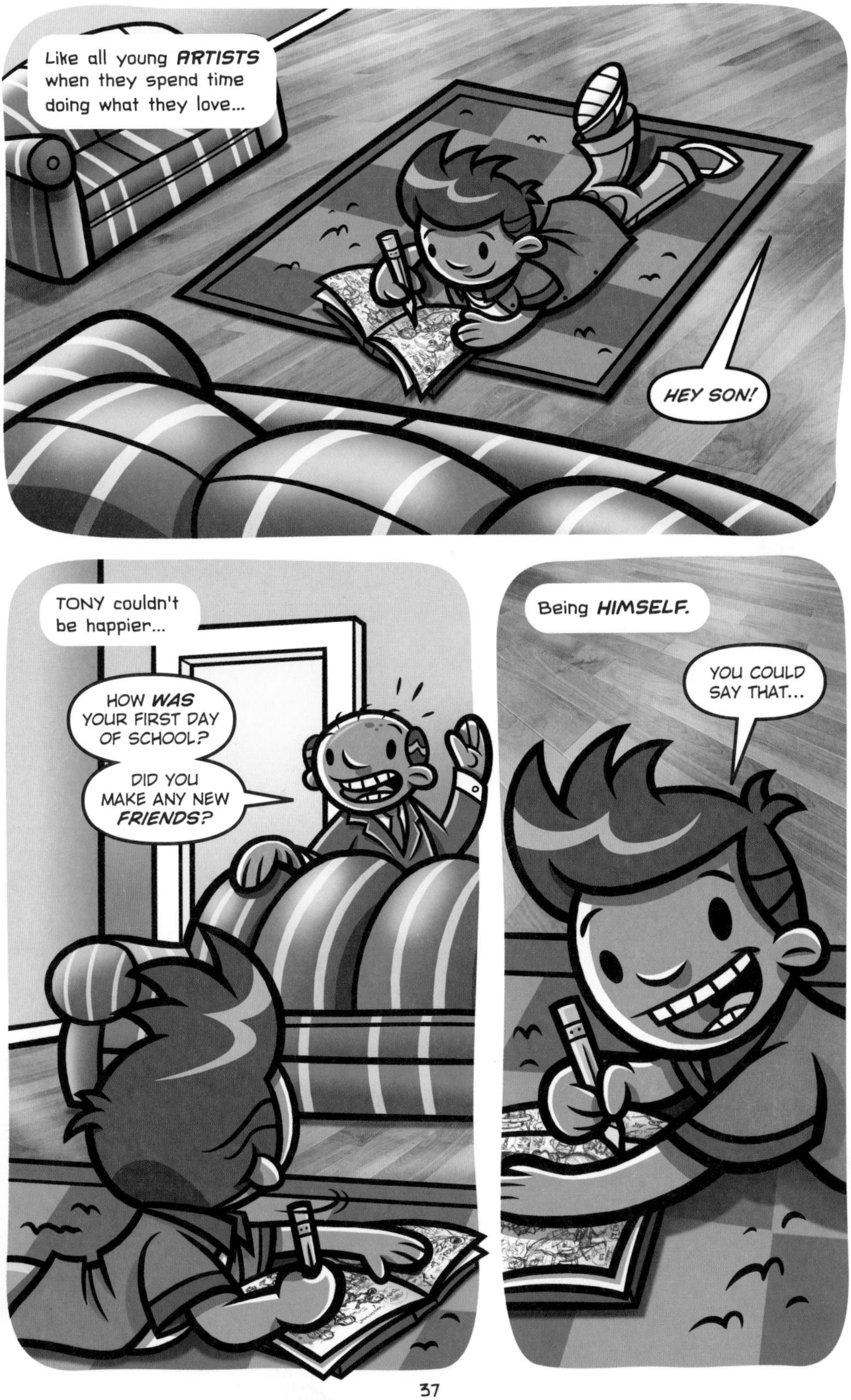
Like all young ARTISTS when they spend time doing what they love...
HEY SON!
TONY couldn't be happier...
HOW WAS YOUR FIRST DAY OF SCHOOL?
DID YOU MAKE ANY NEW FRIENDS?
Being HIMSELF.
YOU COULD SAY THAT...

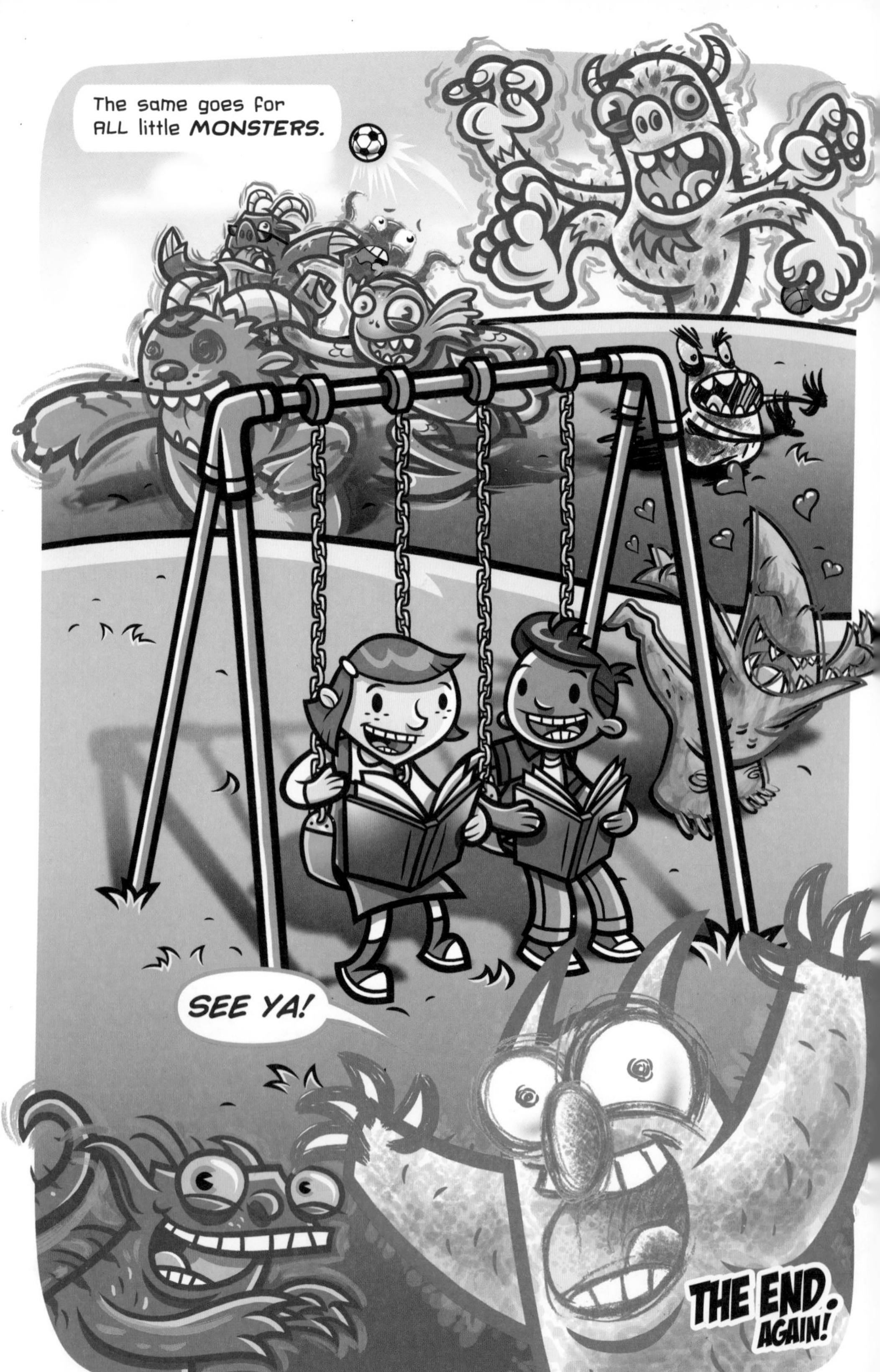
The same goes for
ALL little MONSTERS.
SEE YA!
THE END.
AGAIN!

SKETCHIN' SKETCH MONSTERS

For Sketch Monsters: The New Kid, Vinny had a whole new cast of characters to design! There was Tony, Tony's father, and all of Tony's monsters to draw. Once again, Vinny's sketchbook really came in handy for sketching out all the details.

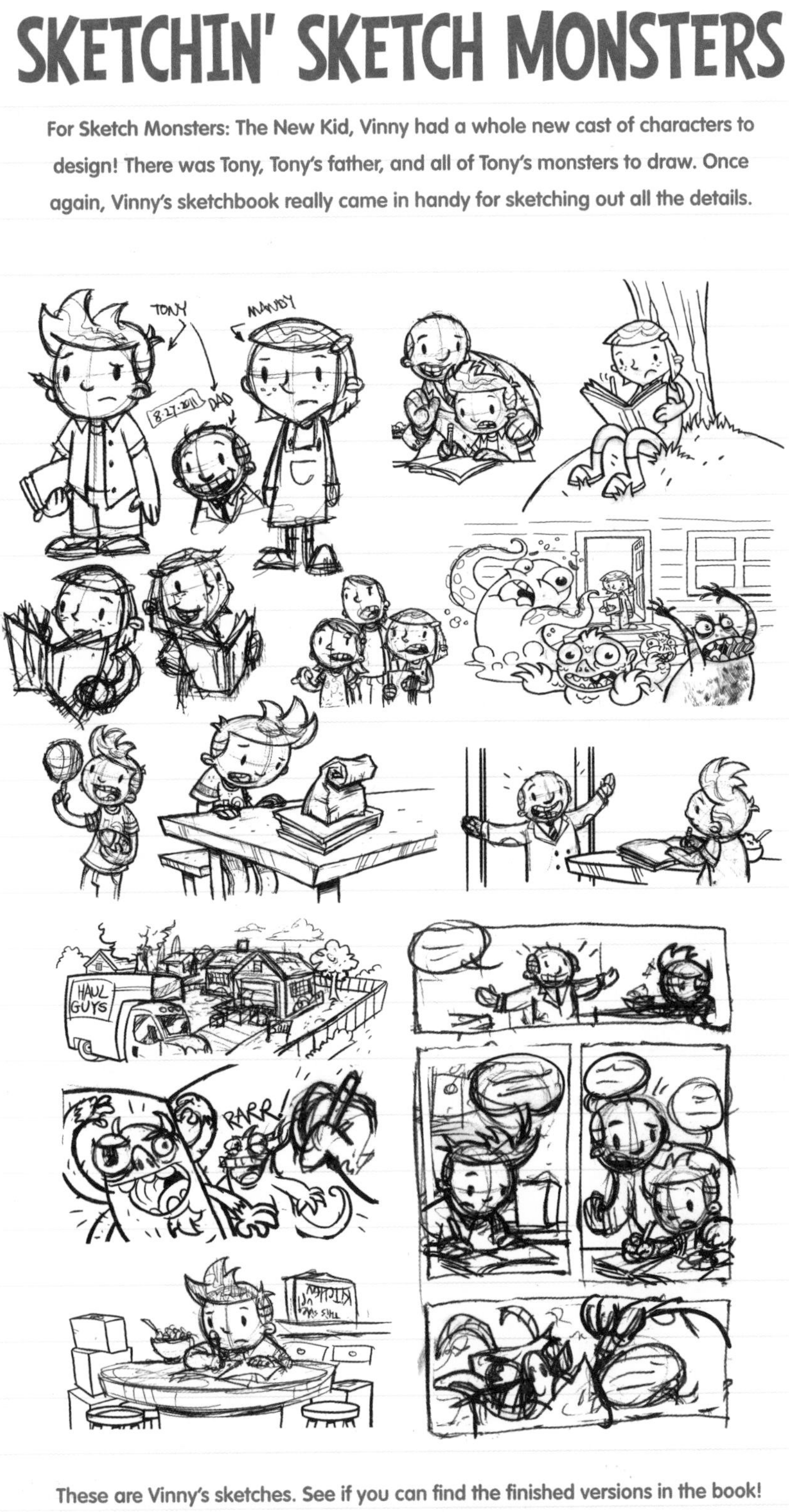
TONY
8·27·2011
DAD
HAUL
GUYS
RARR!

These are Vinny's sketches. See if you can find the finished versions in the book!

Tony was able to catch all of his monsters with help from his new friend, Mandy. Now you can help Tony get through this maze and to his sketchbook! Make sure he collects his monsters on the way!

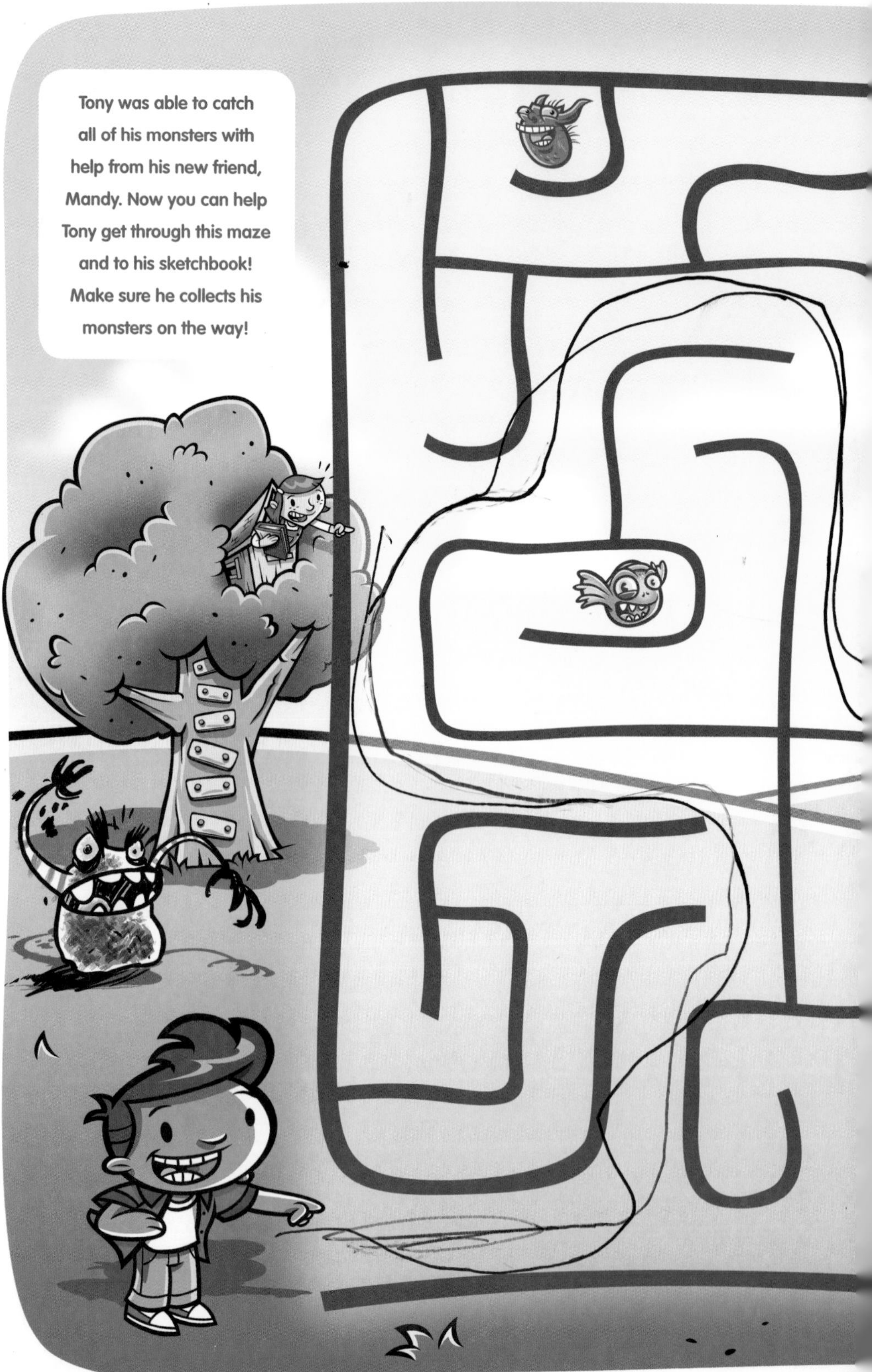

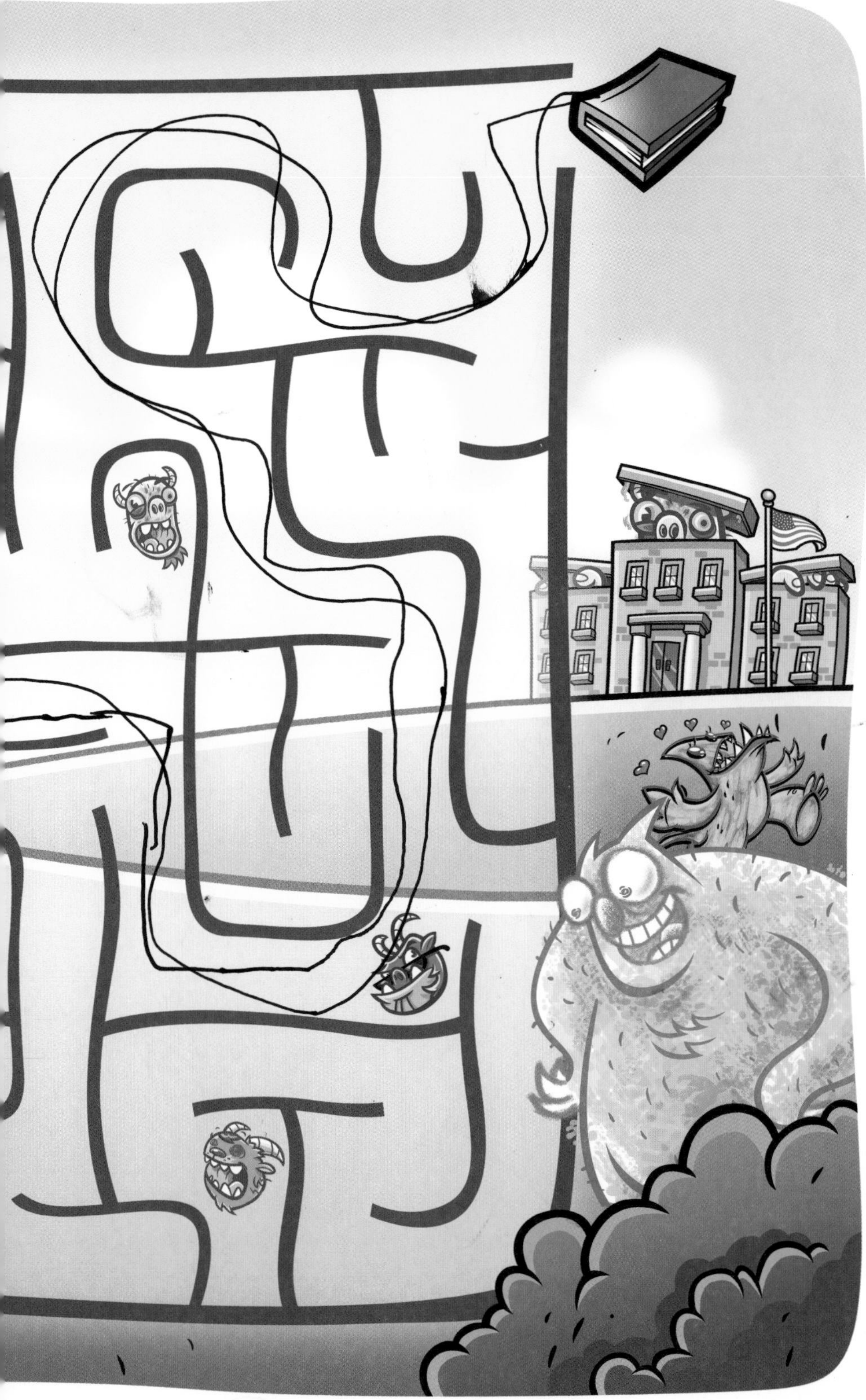

Below are some of the possible character designs for Tony that Vinny drew for this volume. Can you spot the final character design he decided to use for the book?

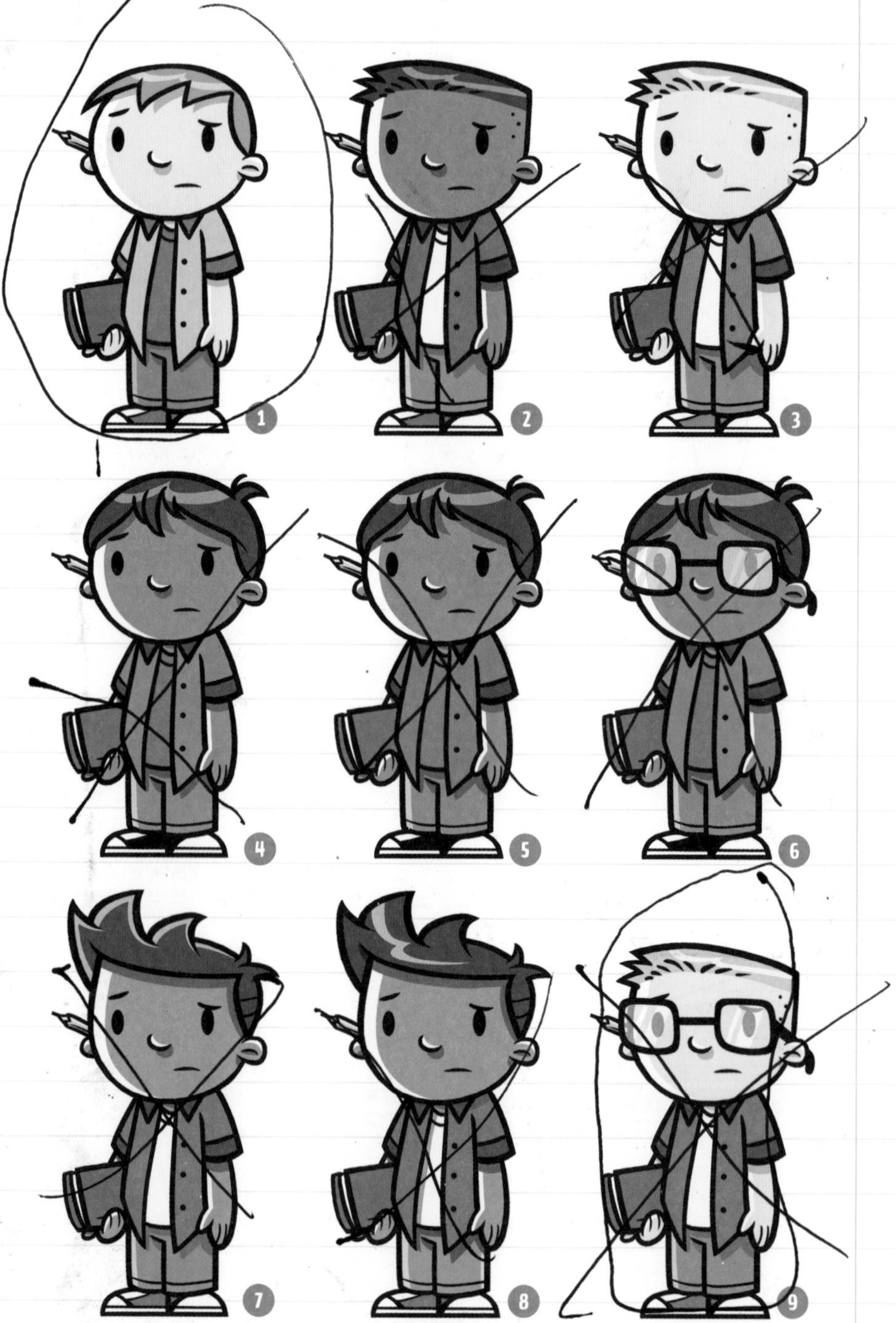
1
2
3
4
5
6
7
8
9

Answer: Number 8!

ABOUT THE AUTHORS

www.thejoshuawilliamson.com

JOSHUA WILLIAMSON writes comics, kids books and resides in Portland, OR, home of big trees, rain and great beer. Williamson has written for a wide variety of publishers and titles including DC Comics' Voodoo, and Superman/Batman, Marvel's Incredible Hulk, Image Comics' Dear Dracula and Xenoholics, and Sketch Monsters for Oni Press. Williamson recently completed writing the tie-in miniseries for Uncharted, the hit PS3 video game, from DC Comics. Joshua writes comics because he can't sing or dance.

Follow him on twitter @Williamson_Josh.

www.vinnyville.carbonmade.com

VICENTE "VINNY" NAVARRETE was born in the Oregon wilderness during the same year Magic and Bird entered the NBA. Vinny himself does not play in the NBA, but does shoot hoops around many Portland parks. If you see him out there you should holler and challenge him to a game of one-on-one.

ALSO AVAILABLE!

SKETCH MONSTERS, VOLUME 1:
ESCAPE OF THE SCRIBBLES

By Joshua Williamson, Vinny Navarrete

48 pages • Hardcover • Color • ISBN 978-1-934964-69-9

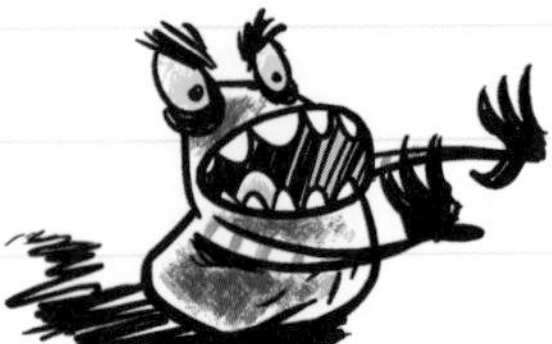

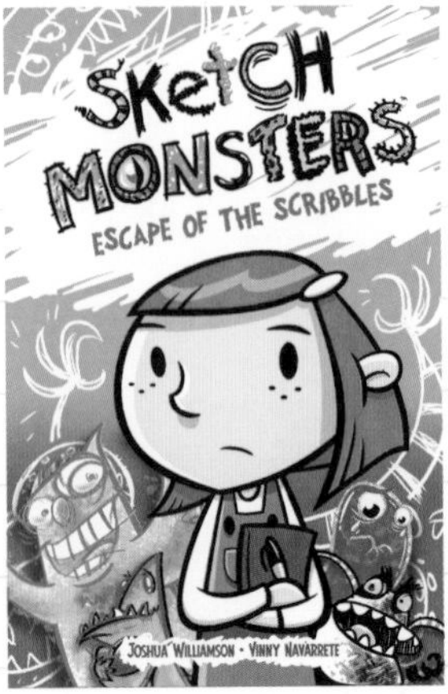
SKETCH MONSTERS
ESCAPE OF THE SCRIBBLES
JOSHUA WILLIAMSON • VINNY NAVARRETE

MORE COMIC BOOKS FOR EARLY READERS!

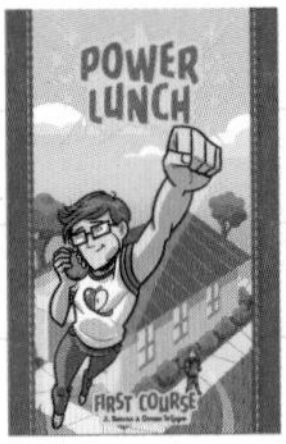
POWER LUNCH
FIRST COURSE

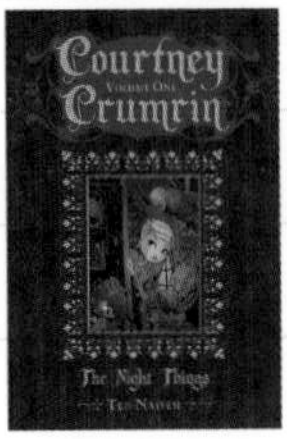
Courtney Crumrin
The Night Things

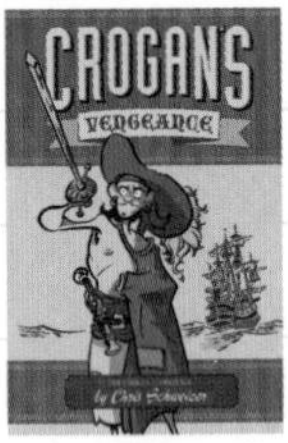
CROGANS
VENGEANCE

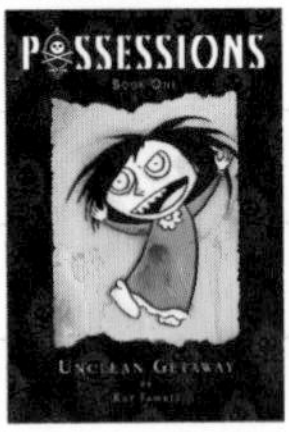
POSSESSIONS
UNCLEAN GETAWAY

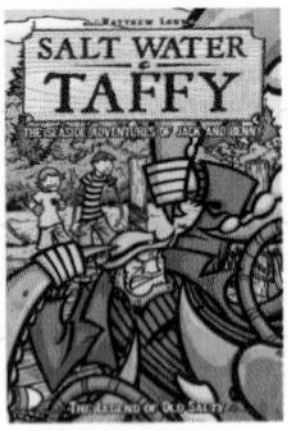
SALT WATER TAFFY

POWER LUNCH, VOLUME 1: FIRST COURSE

By J. Torres & Dean Trippe

40 pages • Color • $12.99 US • 978-1-934964-70-5

COURTNEY CRUMRIN, VOLUME 1: THE NIGHT THINGS

By Ted Naifeh

144 pages • Hardcover • Color • ISBN 978-1-934964-77-4

THE CROGAN ADVENTURES, VOLUME 1: CROGAN'S VENGEANCE

By Chris Schweizer

176 pages • Hardcover • B&W • ISBN 978-934964-06-4

POSSESSIONS, VOLUME 1: UNCLEAN GETAWAY

By Ray Fawkes

88 pages • Digest • Black, Green, and White • $5.99 US • ISBN 978-1-934-964-36-1

SALT WATER TAFFY, VOLUME 1: THE LEGEND OF OLD SALTY

By Matthew Loux

96 pages • Digest • Black and White • $5.95 US • ISBN 978-1-932664-94-2

For more information on these and other fine Oni Press comic books and graphic novels, visit www.onipress.com. To find a comic specialty store in your area, call 1-888-COMICBOOK or visit www.comicshops.us.

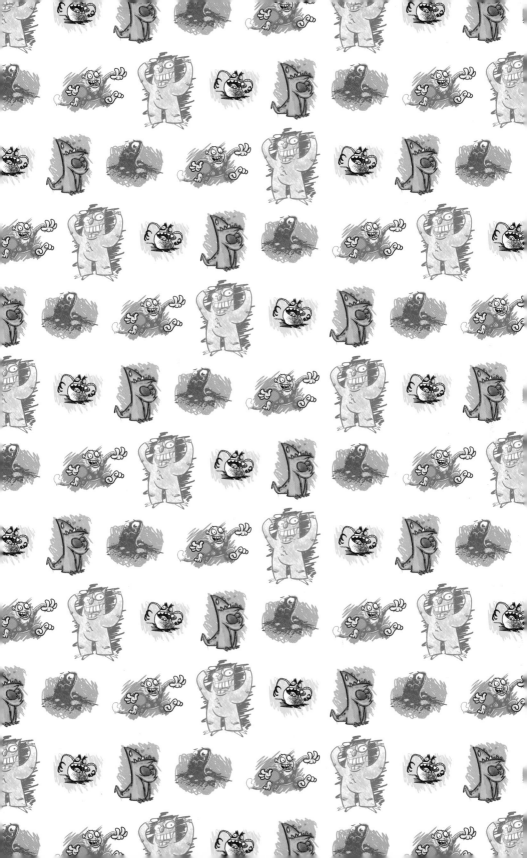

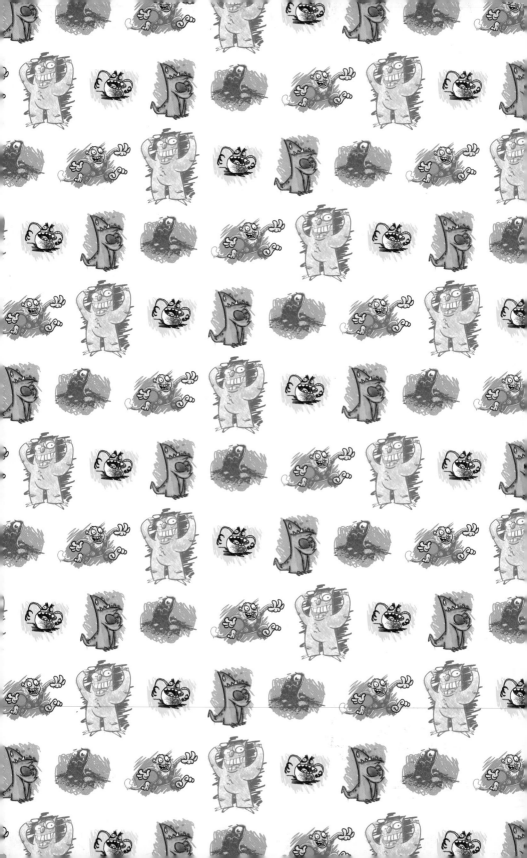